Children's Responses to the Screen

A Media Psychological Approach

Children's Responses to the Screen

A Media Psychological Approach

Patti M. Valkenburg
University of Amsterdam

LAWRENCE ERLBAUM ASSOCIATES, PUBLISHERS
2004   Mahwah, New Jersey   London

Lawrence Erlbaum Associates, Inc., Publishers
10 Industrial Avenue
Mahwah, New Jersey 07430

Cover design by Kathryn Houghtaling Lacey

Library of Congress Cataloging-in-Publication Data

Valkenburg, Patti M., 1958–
    Children's responses to the screen : a media psychological approach /
Patti M. Valkenburg.
        p.   cm.
        Includes bibliographical references and index.
ISBN 0-8058-4763-4 (cloth : alk. paper)
ISBN 0-8058-4764-2 (pbk. : alk. paper)
1. Mass media and children.   I. Title.
HQ784.M3V355   2004
302.23'083—dc22   2003049521
                                                              CIP

Books published by Lawrence Erlbaum Associates are printed on acid-free paper,
and their bindings are chosen for strength and durability.

Printed in the United States of America
10 9 8 7 6 5 4 3 2 1

Contents

Preface

The past few decades have witnessed thousands of studies on children and the media. Yet, much academic research is still in its infancy when it comes to our knowledge about the uses, preferences, and effects of different media. This book provides insight into the latest theories and research on children and the media. As suggested by the title, the book is limited to screen media (i.e., television, films, video and computer games, and the Internet). Verbal media, such as books and the radio, may show up occasionally, but they do not form the primary constituent of this book.

This book is not intended to be a comprehensive textbook on children and the media. Rather, it is concentrated on some fundamental topics that should be included in a media psychology course on children and the media. This choice provides instructors with the opportunity to follow their own teaching preferences and to add supplementary literature to their courses. Each chapter in the book deals with a basic topic on children and the media: the effect of media violence, children's emotional reactions to news and entertainment, the intended and unintended effects of advertising, and the uses and effects of computer games and the Internet.

Each chapter gives an overview of existing theories and research on a particular topic. This general literature review is occasionally illustrated by my own research findings. The book, which is in part a translation of a Dutch book, has been used to accompany lectures at the University of Amsterdam. During my courses, I use the book as a basis and combine it with journal articles reporting empirical research. The student evaluations of the book have always been very positive. In particular, students reported appreciating the combination of a literature review with more concrete examples of empirical research.

Many people have been extremely helpful in the preparation of this book. First of all, I would like to thank my colleagues in the Amsterdam School of Communications Research (ASCoR) for their high-quality comments and suggestions during the writing of the book: Moniek Buijzen, Jeroen Jansz, Joost de Bruin, and Juliette Walma van der Molen.

Of course, generous colleagues are not limited to one research group or university. Joanne Cantor (University of Wisconsin-Madison), Sandra Calvert (Georgetown University), Hans Beentjes (University of Nijmegen), John Sherry (Purdue University), and several anonymous reviewers have also provided very helpful and constructive comments. I am indebted to Mike Newton, who translated several chapters of this book from Dutch into English.

I would also like to acknowledge the Royal Netherlands Academy of Arts and Sciences (KNAW) for providing support by means of a 5-year Royal Academy fellowship in 1997. Without this fellowship, which greatly reduced my teaching load in the past few years, much of the research reported in this book could not have been conducted.

Finally, a different kind of thanks is due to my husband Frank Mauritz. Without his support throughout the process, this book never would have been written.

—Patti Valkenburg

1

Changing Perspectives on Children and the Media

Ever since media started to play a role in children's lives, they have been the subject of heated debates about their positive and negative effects. This first chapter gives a historical overview of the prevailing perspectives on children and the media in the past two centuries. It is comprised of three sections. The first section outlines the change in ideas about childhood from the 18th century to the present. As will become clear, not only have the ideas about media aimed at children changed, but also the views on childhood itself have undergone great shifts that continue even to the present day. The second section reviews the development of empirical research into children and the media. This research, which initially started out of concern for any possible harmful effects of media, has seen a rapid development, particularly since the 1970s. This is in part due to the rise of cognitive psychology, the developing paradigm of the active child, and the increased interest in children on the part of critical researchers. The third and final section gives a preview of the following five chapters of this book.

PERSPECTIVES ON MEDIA AND CHILDHOOD
SINCE THE 18TH CENTURY

Over the past few decades, media aimed specifically at children have developed at a staggering rate. Not only have the number of television channels for children multiplied, but also computer games and the Internet have become an increasingly important part of children's leisure activities. American children between the ages of 2 and 18 years spend on average 5.5 hours a day with some form of media (Roberts, Foehr, Rideout, & Brodie, 1999).

This extensive media use of today's children is all the more remarkable considering that media geared at children is a very recent phenomenon. Historical research has shown that, until the late 18th century, there had been no deliberate attempts at developing media specifically aimed at or intended for children. There were books for adults that children enjoyed reading, such as *Robinson Crusoe* (1719) and *Gulliver's Travels* (1726), but no books were written with a child's cognitive and emotional level in mind (Meigs, 1969).

Until the 18th century, children and adults who could read perused the same texts: the bible, chapbooks and, occasionally, newspapers. The books dealt with subjects such as poverty, disease, and death, as well as adultery, drunkenness, and sexuality. The newspapers contained political and military news, as well as sensational news such as terrifying natural disasters, contagious diseases, witch trials, and abnormal births. No attempts were made to protect children from these harsh realities. Children were confronted with what happened in society, rather than educated about it (Ariès, 1962; Cunningham, 1995).

This circumstance slowly began to change around 1770. Schools began to replace newspapers with children's books. Newspapers, which up until then served as inexpensive school material, were believed to be unsuitable for children by the moralistic educationalists of the time. Other common reading material, such as the bible and fairy tales, were adapted to the experience and emotional level of children. Improper passages, such as the bible story of *Daniel and Susanna*, were censored so as not to threaten the innocence of children's souls. Fairy tales such as *Little Red Riding Hood* and *The Frog Prince*, which originally contained nudity and sexuality, were considered bad for children's moral development and were therefore revised (Ariès, 1962; Ghesquiere, 1988).

The measures to censor the printed media for children can not be seen as separate from the general 18th-century Enlightenment ideas. The Enlightenment philosophers based their ideas on their belief that man is by nature good and pure, and that individual differences can be attributed to environmental circumstances. The environment could be a positive, stimulating influence on children, but could also have a negative and destructive effect. The French philosopher Rousseau was one of the first who proclaimed the notion that children should be raised in freedom in a protected environment separate from the distorting influences of the adult world. In his book *Émile ou l'éducation* (1762) Rousseau pleaded for a childhood that is based not on confrontation and conformity, but rather on education. During this education, children should be given the opportunity to discover themselves, without being subjected to the worries and fears of the adult world. Rousseau felt that the happier and the more carefree the childhood, the less suspicion and aggression the children would have as adults.

The phenomenon of childhood, the carefree and happy period between being a baby and becoming an adult, slowly began to take shape in the second half of the 18th century. For the first time in history, childhood was regarded as a period in its own right and not solely a period of preparation for adulthood. Numerous books specifically aimed at children appeared on the market, many of them boring and didactic books meant to teach children obedience and morals. Children were increasingly considered innocent and vulnerable creatures that needed to be raised far from mature society (Cunningham, 1995; Karl, 1995; Meigs, 1969).

Until the late-19th century, however, this new innocent childhood remained the privilege of the aristocracy and the upper middle class. It was not until the introduction of certain social legislation, such as compulsory education and the ban on child labor that occurred in the early 20th-century in the United States and in Europe, that the phenomenon of childhood penetrated all layers of the population. Before these laws came into effect, it was common for working-class children to work long days in the textile industry, glassworks, or shoe factories. The majority of these children (and their parents) did not have access to printed media, simply because they were illiterate. Working-class children usually had such a short life expectancy that their family upbringing was geared to teaching them to deal with pain and preparing them for an early death (Musgrave, 1966).

It was not until 1900 that the concept of childhood, with its ingredients of innocence, carefreeness, fun, and play, spread across all layers of the population. The same growth applied to media developed for children. In 1919, the first American publishing house set up a separate department for children's books. That year also saw the first Children's Book Week. It is not surprising that many authors referred to the late 19th-century and the first decades of the 20th century as the Golden Age of children's books (Karl, 1995; Meigs, 1969).

Is the Carefree Childhood Disappearing?

The carefree childhood flourished in the first half of the 20th century. Children were entirely protected from the reality of daily life. Subjects such as birth, death, sex, and money were not raised in the family. As was the case in the previous century, the printed media for young people consisted mainly of moralizing stories, devoid of any taboo matters. Some books contained naughty behavior, but this was limited to innocent mischief. There were strict rules about what children of certain ages should and should not know (Meigs, 1969; Meyrowitz, 1985).

In the second half of the 20th century, however, the view of the vulnerable and innocent child was the subject of debate once again. Beginning in the 1960s, many people began to feel that it was wrong to show children a dream world, and that it was important to confront children with reality in order to make them aware of their environment. This new view on children was, in large part, inspired by the development of liberation movements of youngsters, such as the hippies, who stood up against the bourgeoisie and claimed their place in society. From that time, a trend developed in which taboos such as sexuality, death, and divorce were introduced and discussed in media aimed at children.

This new liberating trend of confronting children with the reality of the adult world did not continue uncontested. As of 1980, an increasing number of child psychologists and culture critics observed that children were not treated enough as children, and that they were at risk of losing their childhood. Child psychologist Elkind (1981) was one of the first to express this view in his well-known book *The Hurried Child: Growing Up Too Fast Too Soon.* According to Elkind, children are treated too much like small adults. They are rushed through childhood, causing them to reach adulthood too quickly and too soon. Because children have too many things forced on them for which they are not yet prepared emotionally, a pseudosophistication occurs. The excessive trend of treating children as adults too young could, according to Elkind, lead to stress, insecurity, depression, and aggression among children.

Similar views were expressed by communication philosophers. Joshua Meyrowitz (1985) and Neil Postman (1983) agreed that the phenomenon of childhood is disappearing. According to these authors, today's children are being exposed to information that adults have kept from them for centuries. Both authors observed a homogenization or merging of childhood and adulthood: children acting as adults and adults acting as children, not only with regard to clothes, but also with regard to language, behavior, and entertainment preferences. According to Meyrowitz and Postman, the boundary between children and adults has blurred, or even disappeared, because of this homogenization of childhood and adulthood.

In the past few decades, there have indeed been many indications that childhood is changing. These days, 9-year-old children behave in ways that previously were only observed among older adolescents (15- to 18-year-olds). In the world of marketing, this development has led to the discovery of a new target group: the tweenagers or tweens. This market segment consists of 9- to 12-year-olds, whose preferences and consumer behavior in many aspects resemble that of older adolescents. They are no longer interested in toys but prefer products with a social function (music, clothes) and media entertainment, in which the development of social relationships is central (Valkenburg & Cantor, 2000).

Today's children do not only behave more maturely, but they are also more intelligent than their peers from earlier generations. One of the first researchers to observe that the IQ scores of children have been steadily increasing since the 1950s was James Flynn (1987). He compared the scores of the intelligence tests from 1952 to 1982 in 14 countries, including the United States, Germany, France, and the Netherlands. In almost all countries, he observed a significant increase in IQ scores during this period. According to Flynn, these increases can only be due to environmental factors, such as a higher socioeconomic status and better education. Another remarkable explanation that Flynn offered, was "the television and a greater exposure to information stimuli of all sorts" (p. 189).

The Role of Television and the Carefree Childhood

Nobody can deny that, since the 1960s, childhood in western societies has changed a great deal. The question remains how this change can be explained. Most of the aforementioned authors attributed the changes in childhood to the arrival of electronic media, and to television in particular. Elkind (1981) suggests that television programs have much less of a specific target group than other media. Both young and old watch the same television programs and identify with the same media characters. Because television offers children and adults the same identification possibilities, their experiences are homogenized.

Meyrowitz (1985) and Postman (1983), too, believed that the widespread use of television is the cause of the disappearance of childhood. Postman even went as far as saying that the printed press created childhood two centuries ago, and that television has taken it away from children again. Meyrowitz and Postman felt, as did Elkind (1981), that the written word segregates the various ages, whereas television has an integrating function. After all, when there was no television, children did not have independent access to the printed media, either because they could not read or because they could not understand the content. This segregating function of printed media does not exist in television because television content appeals to and is accessible to both young and old viewers (see Buckingham, 2000, for a more extensive discussion).

Various studies conducted during the introduction period of television do indeed reveal that, from the beginning, television was used differently from other media. A study conducted by Maccoby in 1951 shows, for example, that children's preferences for television were not at all limited to children's programs. Schramm, Lyle, and Parker (1961) found that 6- and 7-year-old children spent approximately 40% of their time in front of the television watching adult programs, and 12-year-olds spent no less than 80%. The reason children like to watch adult television programs is that these programs meet their need to orient themselves toward the adult world. In addition, these programs offer children a common experience about subjects that interest them and their contemporaries, making the social interaction with their peers easier. Finally, by watching adult programs, their status among their peers seems to increase (Paik, 2001).

Historical research has shown that the large-scale exposure of children to media content aimed at adults is indeed unique to television. As mentioned earlier, young children have always had difficulty reading texts aimed at adults, either because they could not read or because their understanding of the material was limited. Radio has also segregated target groups more than television. In the 1930s, children listened to the radio approximately two hours a day. Unlike television, children mainly listened to children's programs on the radio, which were broadcast at times suitable for children (Paik, 2001).

Is it correct, then, to attribute the changes in childhood to the media in general or to television in particular? It can not be denied that the changes in childhood run parallel to the rise of television. It also can not be denied that television informs children of issues with which they would not have come into contact in the past. However, this is not reason enough to say that the arrival of television is the cause of the changes in childhood.

Since the 1960s, various other social developments may be responsible for the observed changes in childhood. For a start, there has been an increasing democratization of human relationships in general and family relationships in particular. Not so long ago, upbringing in western families was characterized by authority, obedience, and respect. This has changed greatly during the past few decades. In today's families, understanding, equality, and compromises are the key words. Parents and children negotiate about what can and has to be done, and depending on the outcome of these negotiations the action is decided upon. Today's parents are more indulgent, often feel guilty, and do more to ensure that their children want for nothing. This can be explained through several factors: Parents have higher incomes and better educational levels than ever before; they have fewer children and have them at a later age; and there are more divorced parents and single-parent families (McNeal, 1992). It is unavoidable that the increased indulgence of parents also affects the children's media use. As mentioned earlier, children's interest in media aimed at adults is not new. However, what is new is the fact that parents are more tolerant with regard to the content of the media that they allow their children to be exposed to.

Again, the changes in childhood are also, symbolic of society's changing views regarding children since the 1960s. Changes in childhood, of course, do not occur in a vacuum. The climate has to be right for the change. Since the 1960s, many political, journalistic, and cultural bodies saw need to bring existing norms and ideals up for discussion. One of the social ideals that has been rebelled against is the paradigm of the vulnerable child. Particularly, the traditionally fixed divisions between children and adults and the associated authoritarian power relationships were discussed and reconsidered.

It can be concluded that the changes in childhood did occur at the same time as the arrival of television. Television has certainly played a part, but it can not be regarded as the only cause for these changes. Both the democratization of family relations and the social criticism on the vulnerable child offer, after all, plausible explanations for the changes in childhood. The latter two developments have probably also contributed to the fact that in western societies there is no longer just one dominating view on childhood. There are various views that can be placed on a continuum between two extreme paradigms: one of the vulnerable child and the other of the empowered child. On the one hand, there is still a social group of fervent supporters of the paradigm of the vulnerable child. This view regards children as passive and innocent creatures, who need to be protected from all evil that comes to them, particularly through media. Supporters of this paradigm believe that the effects of media are great and that children are influenced by media in large numbers.

Flatly opposed to the paradigm of the vulnerable child is that of the empowered child. Supporters of this paradigm can be found relatively often in commercial and marketing circles. In this view children are kids, and these kids can stand up for themselves, and are clever, autonomous, and streetwise (Buckingham, 2000). They easily see through any attempt to deceive or manipulate, and they are spoiled and difficult to please. So the views on childhood, and therefore on media aimed at children, are clearly not always impartial or unbiased. Childhood is not only a biologically determined stage of life, but also a social construction that is influenced by historical, social, and economic factors (Cunningham, 1995).

THE HISTORY OF RESEARCH INTO CHILDREN AND MEDIA

Although for centuries there have been concerns and discussions about the effects of media on children, empirical research into this subject only started in the 1960s. Early empirical media research on children was greatly inspired by general effect theories of mass media on the public. These general effects theories arose in the Interbellum period, stirred by analyses of successful propaganda techniques used in the First World War. These early theories, such as Lasswell's (1927), form the basis of how we think today about the effects of mass media on the individual and society. They were based on the premise that mass media had a large and uniform effect and that the public was passive and easy to influence, these theories therefore are called hypodermic needle theories, stimulus–response theories, or theories of uniform effects.

With our current knowledge of media effects, we know that the prewar effect theories were too simplistic. Few researchers still believe that media have a uniform effect on the public. It is now known that the effects of media depend on many other factors, which are related to the content of the media, the viewer, and the context of the exposure. And yet it seems that the first media effect models could be reasonably well applied to the public in the first half of the 20th century, who were probably much more naive and vulnerable to influences from the media than today's public. Historic research shows that in the early days of cinema, around 1900, adult audiences often screamed or even fled the movie theater when watching a train crash or a building collapse (Kirby, 1988). The famous radio play *The War of the Worlds*, which was broadcast in 1938, also illustrates that the early media public let themselves be influenced in a way that is inconceivable today. This radio play, by the author H. G. Wells, was a realistic account of an invasion of North America by extraterrestrials. Fictitious authorities were questioned and eyewitnesses reported on the invasion. Even before the radio broadcast had finished, masses of people had called neighbors and relatives to warn them of the invasion. Many people fled onto the streets in sheer panic, believing that what they had heard was really happening (Cantril, 1940). Strong reactions like these to fictitious media productions are inconceivable today. They illustrate that the public at the time of the first effect theories was considerably more naive and gullible. It is therefore possible that the early effect theories were valid for the period in which they were developed and so adequately described the reality of the first half of the 20th century (Severin & Tankard, 1997).

The idea of the powerful media was the dominant model of media effects until the early 1950s. When empirical research showed then that the effects of media were not so great and universal as was initially believed, the model of uniform effects was replaced by the limited effects model. This model was developed by the American scholar Klapper (1960), among others. Klapper recognized that the influence of media is limited in various aspects. First of all, a media message does not have to reach everybody because among the audience there is not only selective exposure, but also selective perception, memory, and processing. Klapper emphasized that viewers interpret messages in different ways, and that it is improbable that a message has the same effect on each individual.

The model of the limited or selective effects is today the prevailing paradigm in communication science, and also applies to children. In the past 20 years researchers recognize that children, like adults, are not passive receivers. Children are active and motivated users of media, who critically evaluate what they are shown. Modern researchers now also believe that the effects of media on children are dependent on the manner in which the child deals with the media content they are exposed to. It has often been found that the effect on children of media violence is greatest when a child enjoys watching violence in the media, when he or she identifies with the violent main character, or when he or she assumes that the fictitious violence is real.

The Influence of Cognitive Psychology and the Paradigm of the Active Child

The first academic studies into children and media appeared in the early 1960s. These studies focused primarily on how television can affect children's behavior. Research into media effects on cognition and emotion was carried out as early as the 1970s and 1980s. One of the first researchers into the effects of television on behavior was Albert Bandura (1925–present), who designed a series of experiments (e.g., Bandura, 1965) to test his Social Learning Theory. The assumption of this theory, which is discussed further in chapter 3 of this volume, is that children learn behavior in two ways: through direct experience, and by observing the behavior of others. A child examines how other people behave in certain situations and what the consequences are for them. If the consequences are positive, the child will be more inclined to adopt the particular behavior. However, if the consequences are negative, it is unlikely that the child will do so. According to Bandura, these principles work in the same way when children observe the behavior of people in the media.

Bandura's (1973) theory was initially inspired mainly by *behaviorism*, the psychological school that ignores internal mental processes and assumes that the behavior of people is entirely determined by positive and negative influences from the social environment. Bandura based his ideas on the belief that, as was the case in prewar effect theories, the effects of the media were large and uniform. Children were regarded as a *tabula rasa*, a clean slate, who in a passive manner, through the influences from their environment (family, subculture, and mass media), were maneuvered into their social roles. Bandura's theory ignored the insights of selective effect models, which were already known at the time.

The initial stimulus–response approach of media effects on children was discarded in the 1970s and 1980s, by Bandura and others. At that time a greater emphasis arose within communication science and psychology on the active role of the child. This attention to the active child can on the one hand be explained by the rise of the *uses-and-gratifications* tradition, which assumes that media users, including children, actively and selectively look for information and entertainment to satisfy a certain need. On the other hand, the increased attention to the active child was caused by the rise of cognitive psychology, which in the 1960s replaced behaviorism as the dominant school of thought. Cognitive psychologists study how children and adults acquire, organize, remember, and use cognition (read: knowledge) to control their behavior. In contrast to the behaviorists, they focus on the way in which internal cognitive processes can increase, decrease, or change the effect of information from the environment.

One of the best-known cognitive developmental psychologists who influenced American child psychology of the 1970s was the Swiss Jean Piaget (1896–1980). Piaget (1929) tried to explain the behavior of children by using specific hypotheses of their internal cognitive structures, called *schemata*. Piaget assumed that children use these schemata to understand the things they see, hear, smell, and feel. However, because the schemata of children change greatly as they get older, younger and older children respond very differently to information that comes to them through their environment.

Piaget's ideas about the differences in the cognitive structures of children in various phases of their life were widely accepted. The research into children and the media was also highly stimulated and influenced by his insights. The attention of researchers, which had initially focused primarily on the behavior of children, extended to cognitive effects. There was increased focus on variables such as attention, understanding, and memory of the contents of media programs. There was also more systematic attention given to individual differences in the processing of media content. For example, researchers focused on how children's cognitive level influences their attention and emotional reactions to media content, or their ability to see through the persuasive intention of advertising (see Anderson & Levin, 1976; Bryant, Zillmann, & Brown, 1983; Cantor & Sparks, 1984; Collins, 1975; Huston & Wright, 1983; Singer & Singer, 1976; Wartella & Ettema, 1974).

Bandura (1986), one of the first effect researchers, also modified his Social Learning Theory according to the cognitive change in psychology and insights about the active child. In a more modern version, Bandura put greater emphasis on the cognitive and self-regulating processes of children. He no longer felt that media necessarily had an effect, but that the effect was dependent on the characteristics of the media message, the child, and the environment. The assumption of media psychologists that effects on children are conditional and selective is now so widespread that it has to be considered one of the most fundamental paradigms within media effect research.

The Influence of the Critical Tradition

Since the 1980s, the so-called critical tradition or cultural studies began to focus more on children and media. This tradition, which came about in the United Kingdom in the 1960s, has been interested for some time in the everyday use of media by certain social subgroups but initially focused more on teenagers than on children. In the 1980s their interest shifted to children paralleling the global growth in kids' culture.

Researchers in cultural studies are interested in different questions than psychologically oriented researchers. They are particularly concerned with the question of whether various groups of children have the same level of access to culture. In addition, they are interested in children's media preferences and in the relationship between these preferences and their identity. They also put more emphasis on media content. They investigate, for example, how images of women, children, and ethnic minorities are portrayed in popular kids' culture.

Critical researchers seem to be following a contrary development in their view on children and media than are effect researchers. The first critical media researchers generally showed an optimistic view of children and media. This was perhaps a response to the pessimistic assumptions of the first effect researchers. Children were regarded as autonomous beings who, independent of adults, were able to make meaning out of media contents. This positive view was later moderated. The current generation of critical researchers have a more subtle view of the ability of children to make autonomous media choices (see e.g., Buckingham, 2000; Howard, 1998; Kinder, 1999).

It often seems as though cultural studies avoided the research into the effects of media. This is true to a large extent. Certain effects, such as that of media violence on aggressive behavior, have been systematically ignored. A number of other effects, however, have been studied, but under another name. Many of the concepts that psychologically oriented researchers categorize under *effects*, are grouped under the broader concept of *ideology* in the critical tradition. Critical researchers often implicitly investigate effects in their research into the ways in which children reproduce or negotiate the meanings out of media texts (Kinder, 1999; Livingstone, 1998). Some researchers, for example, feel that Disney animated films are teaching machines that form young children's understanding of issues such as patriarchy and racism (Giroux, 1998). Statements that media violence encourages ideologies about patriotism and militarism are also effect claims from the part of cultural studies (McLaren & Morris, 1998). Many of these researchers base their conclusions solely on studying media texts, and not on research into audience responses. Much work in cultural studies is implicitly or explicitly based on the notion that cultural texts have "preferred meanings" that are difficult to resist by the public (Tobin, 2000, p. 5).

Similarities Between the Traditions.   Although critical media researchers are concerned with other research questions, this tradition also shows a number of important similarities with psychologically oriented researchers. One of the similarities is their belief in the active child. Both critical and psychological researchers consider children to be active media consumers, who interpret in their own way the content of media programs that they see. Unfortunately, the concept of the active media consumer causes the same misunderstandings in both traditions. All too often researchers use the concept to imply that active (rather than passive) child viewers are less affected by the media because (according to the effect researchers) they have cognitive defense mechanisms or (according to the critical researchers) they negotiate the meanings of the media content. However, the fact that children are active in the sense that they interpret media in their own way does not necessarily mean that they are less influenced. They can also be more influenced if they actively open up to certain influences.

Another similarity among both traditions is that they recognize that the social context of children determines what children learn through the media. In psychologically oriented research, this is acknowledged in studies into adult mediation. The adult mediation research assumes that the social environment of the child, and particularly the parents, can counteract many media effects on children, for example by offering extra explanation and interpretation or by making critical comments and putting media contents into perspective. In the critical tradition, the influence of children's social environment is covered by the concept of counterdiscourse. It is assumed that children who participate in a social environment, in which they learn to deal critically with certain ideologies, are less susceptible to media contents that proclaim these ideologies (Tobin, 2000).

Although, as earlier mentioned, the critical research tradition has always been characterized by a relatively positive view on children and the media, it is not correct to assume that only psychologically oriented researchers are concerned about the developments in the media culture of children. According to cultural studies researcher Kinder (1999), neither of the two traditions can ignore a number of important issues concerning children and the media. These include the escalation of violence among youngsters, the ever-increasing younger age at which children are regarded as consumers, the mix of challenges and risks on the Internet, and the increased need for policy measures concerning children and media. These subjects deserve empirical research from all research traditions. Most of these subjects will be examined in the remaining chapters of this book.

A PREVIEW OF THE OTHER CHAPTERS

In this chapter, I explained that childhood is not only a phase of life but also a social construction that is influenced by historical, political, and economic factors. I have shown that changes in the ideas about childhood go hand in hand with changes in media content designed for children. I have also shown that the views on children, and on the media aimed at children, have shifted back and forth since the 18th century.

This chapter also briefly outlined the history of research into children and media. Although the subject of children and their media has been debated for centuries, research only really got going after the arrival of television. The first research focused mainly on the behavioral effects of media. Later the research attention shifted to cognitive and emotional effects, and there came more interest in children's media preferences. This shift in the focus of the research was caused by the rise of cognitive psychology, the paradigm of the active child, and the increasing interest in kids' culture from critical media researchers.

This book comprises six chapters, which together offer an insight into the most important subjects in the research into children and media. The next chapter, chapter 2, offers insight into the way in which children develop into media consumers. It describes a number of important characteristics of children that determine their preferences for the content of media programs, such as the cognitive developmental level of children as well as their gender. This chapter shows why children can not be regarded as a homogenous target group. Children can differ as much from each other as they differ from adults. As will become clear later, effects can be very different for boys than for girls, for younger than for older children, and for children from families with different levels of education.

The third chapter of this book discusses a subject that within media research has traditionally received the most attention: the effect of media violence on aggressive behavior. This chapter deals with the most important theories about the influence of media violence, such as the social learning theory, cognitive script theory, arousal theory, and desensitization theory. It also examines the various types of research that have been carried out so far and how these have contributed to our knowledge of the effect of media violence on aggression. Finally, this chapter describes which children are particularly sensitive to media violence and how potential effects on these children can be reduced.

The fourth chapter describes fear responses of children to news and entertainment. This chapter examines questions such as: How often do children get scared when seeing certain television programs; and when do these fears start and how do they develop as these children get older? It deals with various theories that explain why children get scared when watching programs that actually do not pose a threat to them. Then it examines how children comfort themselves when they become scared and how these comfort strategies change as children get older. And finally, chapter 4 discusses a number of theories that explain why children enjoy watching media violence, even when it frightens them.

The fifth chapter focuses on children and advertising. This chapter begins with the question of how children's brand awareness develops and what kinds of influence children have on family purchases. It then discusses the effects of advertising on children. It will become clear that advertising does not have just one but rather several effects, and that there is therefore no point in discussing the effect of advertising. The effects of advertising are often divided into *intended* and *unintended* effects. Intended effects are effects that advertisers wish to achieve with their advertisements. These are effects on, for example, the brand awareness, brand attitude, and purchase intention of children. Unintended effects are undesired side effects of advertising such as family conflict and materialism. Both types of effects are discussed in this chapter. The chapter also reviews a number of characteristics of advertising, such as repeating commercials, the use of celebrity endorsement, and the use of visual cues on packaging, which, it is assumed, reinforce one or more of these effects on children. Finally, the question of which children are most susceptible to the various effects of advertising will be discussed. Research has shown, for example, that young children are more susceptible than older children to the effects of advertising on brand attitude. Chapter 5 will provide explanations for these findings.

The sixth and final chapter deals with interactive media and computer games and the Internet in particular. Over the past few years, the use of interactive media has grown enormously among children. The chapter begins with a description of the interactive media environment of children. It discusses a number of characteristic features of Web sites for children as well as the various types of computer and web games that are available. After that the chapter explores the key question of which children use interactive media and how this differs for boys and girls of different age groups and backgrounds. And finally, it describes a number of positive and negative effects of interactive media. It discusses the most important physical (epileptic seizures), cognitive (spatial awareness), and social effects (friendships and aggression) of interactive media.

2

The Development of a Child
Into a Media Consumer

Most people seem to agree that children have distinct tastes when it comes to consuming media entertainment. This chapter reviews how children's media preferences develop from infancy to adolescence. The chapter consists of five sections. The first four sections focus on the specific media preferences of four different age groups: birth to 2 years, 2 to 5 years, 5 to 8 years, and 8 to 12 years. In each of these four sections, it is argued how some developmental-psychological characteristics of children predict their preferences for entertainment and media content. Why, for example, do 2- and 3-year-olds like to watch slow programs with lots of repetition, whereas 5-year-olds go for adventure? Which types of humor appeal to children of different ages and why? Why do children see through bad acting as early as the age of 8? The fifth and final section deals with some important differences between the media preferences of boys and of girls. In this section, it is explained how boys and girls differ in their preference for humor, action, violence, and romance. Finally, it provides a number of explanations for these gender differences.

COGNITIVE-DEVELOPMENTAL LEVEL AND CHILDREN'S
PREFERENCES FOR MEDIA CONTENT

When television researchers became interested in the cognitive effects (e.g., attention, comprehension) of television in the 1970s, they initially embraced the reactive model of television viewing (Anderson & Pugzles-Lorch, 1983). Adherents of this model assume that children's attention to television is passively directed by salient program features, such as sound effects, rapid char-

15

acter action, and special camera techniques (e.g., Singer, 1980). If these features are successfully employed by television producers, children's attention to the screen is guaranteed, and their comprehension and retention automatically follow. In short, the reactive model of television viewing argues that the direction of influence points from program features to attention and comprehension (for a discussion see Anderson & Pugzles-Lorch, 1983; Huston & Wright, 1983).

In the 1980s, however, the reactive model of cognitive television effects was increasingly criticized, in part due to some pioneering studies by Daniel Anderson and colleagues (e.g., Anderson, Pugzles-Lorch, Field, & Sanders, 1981; Pugzles-Lorch, Anderson, & Levin, 1979). These researchers demonstrated that young children's attention to television was not exclusively determined by salient program features. They found, for example, that when children did not understand television content, their attention to the screen reduced. A series of subsequent studies confirmed that children's attention to the screen was a result of a confluence of factors, including program comprehensibility (Campbell, Wright, & Huston, 1986; Pingree, 1986), cognitive-developmental level of the child (Calvert, Huston, Watkins, & Wright, 1982; Huston, Wright, Rice, Kerkman, & St. Peters, 1990), and program features (Alwitt, Anderson, Pugzles-Lorch, & Levin, 1980). These research results led to a fundamentally different perspective on young children's television watching. It was recognized that children use their comprehension schemata (their existing knowledge and understanding) to direct their attention to television content. Rather than being reactive viewers, children came to be seen as active explorers of television content. In this new, active model of television viewing, the direction of influence points from comprehension to attention and liking, and not the other way around (Anderson & Pugzles-Lorch, 1983; Bickham, Wright, & Huston, 2001).

Attention, Liking, and Stimulus Complexity

In the past decades, several media-effects researchers have suggested that the concept of optimal level of stimulation (Berlyne, 1971) might be central to understanding young children's attention to television (Anderson & Pugzles-Lorch, 1983; Bickham et al., 2001; Husson, 1982; Huston & Wright, 1983; Watts & Welch, 1983). These authors assume that young children prefer to look at stimuli that they can at least partially incorporate into their existing comprehension schemata, and that they show less preference for extremely simple or extremely complex stimuli. This *moderate-discrepancy hypothesis* (McCall, Kennedy, & Applebaum, 1977) predicts that at any given age, a moderate level of stimulus complexity is preferred and that this level increases as the child matures.

The moderate-discrepancy hypothesis predicts an inverted U-shaped rela-tion between program comprehensibility and attention: Children's attention should be highest for television content that departs only slightly from what they know or are capable of (Anderson & Pugzles-Lorch 1983; Bickham et al., 2001; Huston & Wright, 1983). The moderate-discrepancy hypothesis offers a viable explanation of why the media preferences of children in various age groups differ so greatly. After all, the perceived simplicity and complexity of media content changes dramatically as children mature. Media content that is only moderately discrepant and therefore attractive to 2-year-olds may be overly simple and thus unattractive to 6-year-olds. Later in this chapter, it be-comes clear that many developments in children's media preferences can be explained by the moderate-discrepancy hypothesis.

INFANTS AND TODDLERS (AGE 0–2):
BRIGHT COLORS, MUSIC, AND MOVING OBJECTS

Researchers know little about how children's tastes and preferences are formed during childhood. They do know, however, that even toddlers are able to firmly express their tastes and preferences regarding their favorite food, toys, televi-sion programs, and home videos. It is also known that, as they mature, children are progressively able to voice sophisticated and critical views about media pro-ductions.

Some tastes and preferences of children seem to be innate, whereas others are formed during childhood. For example, children's preferences for tastes and smells are largely inborn. Newborns typically prefer sweet substances, and they do not like salty, sour, or bitter liquids. They have also been shown to dis-like the same smells that adults consider disagreeable, such as vinegar and am-monia (Ganchrow, Steiner, & Daher, 1983).

Children are also born with a specific preference for music and speech. Al-ready in the first few months, they start to turn their head toward the source of music, and they have been observed listening to music with an unmistakable ex-pression of enjoyment (Moog, 1976). Another favorite sound for newborns is the human voice—especially a human voice using a form of speech known as *motherese*, which is characterized by a slower pace, a higher pitch, and greatly ex-aggerated intonations. It has been shown that infants as young as 4 months clearly prefer tape-recorded speech in motherese to speech in standard intona-tions (Fernald, 1985). This preference for motherese lasts for several years. Audio or audiovisual stories for this age group that use this type of speech therefore have a greater chance of success.

Although infants are quite responsive to music and speech, their visual abili-ties still have to come to full bloom. Newborns are able to see colors, contrasts, and movements, but the images they see are still somewhat blurred. It is at around 8 months that their visual ability is comparable to that of adults. Still, from the day they are born, infants have a preference for very specific images. They prefer to look at moving objects with bright (but not too bright) colors and sharp contrasts. Immediately after birth, they can distinguish between different colors, and when they are 1 month old, they are able to discern all colors in the spectrum (Adams, 1987; Clavadetscher, Brown, Ankrum, & Teller, 1988). It is no coincidence, therefore, that many toys and media productions for infants and toddlers are produced in such colors.

Infants' Attention to Television Programs

When children are 4 to 5 months of age, they start to pay attention to television programs. They are mostly interested in preschool programs with brightly colored fantasy puppets and commercials (Lemish, 1987). The finding that infants and toddlers are attracted to commercials sometimes surprises and even worries parents. However, this knowledge is certainly not new. In 1969, for example, it induced the producers of *Sesame Street* to develop the program in a format similar to that of commercials: short stories and an abundant use of music, slogans, rhymes, and songs (Lesser, 1974).

Both preschool programs and commercials specialize in drawing attention by visual and auditory stimuli, and, because of their specific attention system, infants are very sensitive to these types of programs. According to Ruff and Rothbart (1996), the first year of life is characterized by a system of attention, which is referred to as the investigative/orienting system. In this period, infants primarily orient to novel or otherwise salient stimuli. They sustain attention to those stimuli for the purpose of exploring and learning. As the child develops into a toddler, his or her selectivity becomes less influenced by novelty and more by what is intrinsically interesting to him or her.

The specific preference of infants for visual and auditive attributes in television programs has been confirmed in an observational study of ours, in which we observed fifty 6- to 48-month-olds while they were watching television in their natural home situation. In reality, their television viewing was a 40-minute videotape, consisting of program segments from the news, *Sesame Street*, *Teletubbies*, and *Lion King II*. Between the program segments, several commercials were shown, for example, for coffee, a washing powder, Barbie, and Winnie the Pooh (Valkenburg & Vroone, 2004).

We started our study with an analysis of the attributes that program developers use to stimulate young children's attention. To this end, we divided the program segments into 64 scenes, and coded each of these scenes on 36 visual, auditory, and content attributes that may stimulate young children's attention and liking. These attributes were derived from television research into young children's attention to and preferences for media content (e.g., Alwitt et al.,

1980; Anderson & Levin, 1976; Lemish, 1987; Valkenburg & Cantor, 2000). The 36 attributes that may stimulate children's attention to and liking of television programs are listed in Table 2.1.

By means of a small video camera placed on top of the television set, we were able to assess the extent to which children paid attention to each of the 64 successive scenes. Table 2.2 presents the three scenes, and their auditory, visual, and content attributes, that drew the most attention from 6- to 18-month-old children.

The favorite scenes of 6- to 18-month-olds were all characterized by an abundance of salient visual and auditory attributes. For example, the most

TABLE 2.1

Program Attributes That Stimulate Children's Attention To and Liking of Television Content

Auditory	Visual	Meaningful Content
Adult female voice	Adult female	Food/candies
Animated dialogue	Animal	Letters/numbers
Animated voice	Affection/snuggle	Instructional speech
Applause	Animated character	Meaningful dialogue
Auditory repetition	Baby	Play
Baby sound	Bright colors	Verbal humor
Child voice	Cartoon character	
Laughter	Chase/pursuit	
Music	Child	
Peculiar sound	Dancing	
Singing	Moderate character movement	
	Physical humor	
	Rapid character movement	
	Special camera technique	
	Special visual effect	
	Toys	
	Transformation	
	Visual repetition	
	Visual surprise	

Note. Adapted from Valkenburg and Vroone, 2004.

TABLE 2.2

The Three Television Scenes That Drew the Most Attention
from Children Aged 6 to 18 Months

	Program Attributes Present in Scene		
Scene Description	*Auditory*	*Visual*	*Meaningful Content*
Opening scene Sesame Street	Applause/cheering	Adult female	
	Auditory repetition	Animated character	Play
	Child voice	Bright colors	
	Laughter	Child	
	Music	Dancing	
	Singing	Physical humor	
		Rapid character action	
		Special visual effects	
		Toys	
		Transformation	
		Visual surprise	
Teletubbies shower head: "Time for Teletubbies, Time for Teletubbies"	Applause/cheering	Animated character	
	Auditory repetition	Bright colors	Play
	Child voice	Dancing	
	Laughter	Physical humor	
	Music	Rapid character action	
	Peculiar sound	Special visual effects	
	Singing	Visual surprise	
Teletubbies dancing and singing	Applause/cheering	Affection/snuggle	
	Auditory repetition	Animated character	
	Child voice	Bright colors	
	Laughter	Dancing	
	Music	Rapid character action	
	Peculiar sound		
	Singing		

Note. Adapted from Valkenburg and Vroone, 2004.

popular scenes all contained laughter, applause, and cheering. They also all contained auditory repetition, music, singing, bright colors, dancing, and rapid character action. The scenes illustrate that children of this age group react strongly to salient visual and auditory attributes of television programs and hardly react to meaningful content attributes.

There were many scenes that drew little or no attention in this age group. The news, for example, received attention from only 8% of the children. In addition, not one commercial aimed at adults ranked among the children's favorite scenes, nor—remarkably—did any scene from the adventurous, fast-paced *Lion King II*. These results confirm developmental theories on attention, which suggest that infants are highly selective in their attention to television content. Our results also seem to be in agreement with the moderate-discrepancy hypothesis. The news, the commercials aimed at adults, and *Lion King II* all consisted of relatively difficult scenes for this age group, which may explain why they attracted relatively little attention (Valkenburg & Vroone, 2004).

Conclusion. Even infants and toddlers have specific preferences for auditory and visual attributes of television programs (e.g., Alwitt et al., 1981; Calvert et al., 1982; Campbell et al., 1987). In line with the active model on television viewing our study showed that television viewing is not a passive activity for young children. Children in our study tended to be cognitively and physically very active while watching. However, the infants and toddlers in our study did not yet have an eye for the story line of the media productions. They seemed to react to auditory and visual attributes, such as songs, bright colors, and objects, but they did not show any signs that they understood the story line. This finding is in line with earlier research that has shown that although infants and toddlers certainly have an eye for salient visual and auditory program attributes, these attributes do not yet have to occur in a meaningful context (e.g., Richards & Gibson, 1997).

PRESCHOOLERS (AGE 2–5): FRIENDLY FANTASY CHARACTERS AND FAMILIAR CONTEXTS

Although infants and toddlers have distinct preferences for colors, images, sounds, and music, their behavior is still primarily reactive and not very intentional. However, this changes very rapidly as children become 2 years of age. At this time they start to actively express their preferences for media content. In our observation study, 28% of the toddlers and preschoolers spontaneously communicated their likes and dislikes of certain television content. This active expression of their media preferences started at around 30 months:

> Girl (30 months) watching a Barbie commercial: "This one is cool mama, this one is cool!"

Boy (33 months) watching *Lion King*: "I don't want Lion on!"
Boys (35 months) watching coffee commercial: "I want to see Bert and Ernie!"
Girl (50 months) watching the news: "Yuck!"
Boy (56 months) watching *Teletubbies*: "I want to play tennis, I don't like this!"

Around 2 years of age, most children watch television on a daily basis and from this age their attention to program content increases dramatically. A study by Anderson, Pugzles-Lorch, Field, Collins, and Nathan (1986) demonstrated that 1-year-old children have their eyes on the screen for only 12% of the time a television is on, whereas for 5-year-olds this figure has increased to 70% (the apparent maximum, because the average time that older children have their eyes on the screen fluctuates around this percentage).

According to Anderson and colleagues (1986), the rapid increase in attention to television programs between 1 and 5 years of age reflects the proportionally rapid increase in children's understanding of television content. The vocabulary of children increases noticeably during this period. It has been estimated that, an average 2-year-old has only a few hundred words at his or her disposal, whereas an average 6-year-old knows around 10,000 words. As discussed earlier, from 2 years on, children start to develop a genuine interest in the storyline of media productions. In our observation study, children's interest in the storyline could be deduced from the nature and frequency with which they asked questions about a program. Almost one half of the children asked the researcher questions in order to improve their understanding of the program's content. This asking of questions started at around the age of 2½ years.

Imitating Media Contents

From the moment they are born, children are able to imitate other people (Siegler, 1998). However, they start to recognize themselves in a mirror or a photo only when they reach the age of 18 months. Then they start to understand how people differ from each other and start to really enjoy imitating other people, including media characters. In a study by Cupitt, Jenkinson, Ungerer, and Waters (1998), almost one half of the mothers of a 2½-year-old child reported that their child had imitated music, rhymes, or songs from television. Commercials especially seem to be often imitated by children. In one of our survey studies, 25% of the parents of 2-year-olds indicated that their child had imitated a song, slogan, or jingle from a commercial. This percentage rapidly increased: Sixty-three percent of parents of 3-year-olds and 75% of parents of 5-year-olds reported that their child had more or less regularly imitated songs, slogans, or jingles from commercials (Valkenburg, 1999).

Why a Slow Pace and Lots of Repetition?

Because of their early cognitive capacities, much information presented to young children is beyond their existing knowledge and experiences. According to the moderate-discrepancy hypothesis, much information presented to young children must therefore be categorized as *too complex*. Younger children have less prior knowledge and fewer experiences than older children to help them select, order, and process new information. It is no surprise, then, that they usually need more time than older children to interpret and make sense of television images. This is why many young preschoolers like to watch programs with a slow pace and lots of repetition, and why they are usually not attracted to fast-paced programs with rapidly changing images (Anderson & Burns, 1991). A good example of a slow-paced program is *Teletubbies*. Although this program may irritate some adults, it is pre-eminently suited to the taste of toddlers and young preschoolers. Programs with lots of repetition offer children the opportunity to develop a kind of psychological mastery over the stories. Just like adults need some time to master difficult material by rereading it several times, toddlers gain a kind of psychological mastery over difficult (or initially upsetting) scenes by watching them repeatedly.

The moderate-discrepancy hypothesis also explains why toddlers and preschoolers prefer to watch programs with familiar contexts, that is, programs with situations they recognize and that occur close to home. They prefer to watch other toddlers and preschoolers and simple, nonthreatening fantasy characters. They also have a special interest in familiar objects and animals that they can label verbally, like a dog, cat, or bird—which is why many storybooks and television programs for young preschoolers use familiar contexts, such as a home, farm, or day-care center. Children in this age group still like to listen to music, songs, and rhymes. Appropriate forms of humor for this age group are physical and visual forms of humor, such as sudden surprises, clownish gestures, and slapstick (Valkenburg & Cantor, 2000).

The Blurred Boundary Between Fantasy and Reality

Between the ages of 2 and 5, children's fantasy develops exponentially. The first utterances of fantasy usually start at the age of 18 months. At that time, children are able to pretend that a banana is a telephone. When they are 3 or 4, their fantasy play becomes progressively complex and social. Children are able to adopt different roles and they can think up and play out complex play scenarios. They

play mothers and fathers, and doctors and firemen, and they sail off to uninhab-
ited islands and remote planets.

Early theories of cognitive development assumed that children are not able
to distinguish between fantasy and reality until they are 6 years old. Piaget
(1929), for example, assumed that children younger than 6 have no apprecia-
tion of mental life at all. He believed that young children can not distinguish between thoughts, dreams, and real physical things. However, more recent
research shows that even 3-year-olds are reasonably capable of appreciating the
fantasy–reality distinction (Wellman, 1990). The following discussion between a mother and her 3-year-old daughter in Astington (1993) illustrates this
capability of children:

Mother:	"What shall we have for dinner?"
Katie:	"Daddy."
Mother:	"That's a good idea, yes, with ketchup."
Katie:	"Let's have Mommy for dinner."
Mother:	"With Ketchup?"
Katie:	"Yes."
Mother:	"But then Mommy would be eaten all up. I'd be all gone if you had me for dinner."
Katie:	(looking upset) "… It's just pretend." [1]

Although experimental research has demonstrated that preschoolers understand
pretense, everyday practice often provides a quite different picture. Research into
the validity of eyewitness testimonies, for example, often demonstrates that, even
with the most valid research methods, preschoolers have more difficulty than
older children in reality monitoring, that is, distinguishing what they imagined
from what really happened (Parker, 1995; Siegler, 1998). Many adults know all too
well that a child's knowledge that a film like *The Wizard of Oz* is "just pretend" does
not preclude that child from being terrified by the flying monkeys in this film
(Davies, 1997). According to Paul Harris (2000), these children know that this film
is fantasy, but they still are more inclined than older children and adults to believe
in their own fantasies and those of others. Harris qualified the boundary between
fantasy and reality therefore as semipermeable. The following piece of dialogue
clearly illustrates the assumption that the boundary between fantasy and reality is
still not clearly drawn in preschoolers:

"Pretend there's a monster coming, OK?"
"No, let's don't pretend that."
"OK, why?"
"Cause it's too scary, that's why." [2]

---

[1]From Astington (1993).
[2]From Carvey and Berndt, cited in Astington (1993).

Fantasy–Reality Distinction and Media Preferences.   In the previous sections, it became clear that young children have a reasonable knowledge of their own and of other's pretense but that their ability to distinguish between fantasy and reality is less developed when they have to think of the past and when they are confronted with fear-provoking situations and images. However, it is still not clear how children of different ages react to fantasy portrayals in the media. At what age are children capable of distinguishing between fantasy and reality in media productions? Research has shown that between the ages of 3 and 10, children gradually become more accurate in distinguishing fantasy from reality on television. Until they are 4, children believe that everything on television is real. Young preschoolers sometimes even think that television characters live inside the TV set (Noble, 1975). Two- to three-year-olds have been observed running to the kitchen to get a paper towel after seeing an egg breaking on television (Jaglom & Gardner, 1981). Howard (1998) found that most 4-year-olds in her study were convinced that Big Bird and Bugs Bunny are real.

The finding that preschoolers do not yet understand that some television content is unrealistic is clearly expressed in their behavior. When young children like a certain television character, they may walk to the screen, for example, to pet or kiss the character. According to Lemish (1987), this touching of the screen disappears by 2 years of age because by then children have learned that the screen feels the same (cold and flat) every time it is touched. Our observation study showed, however, that many 3-year-olds still walk to the screen, for example to wave at their favorite television characters or to grab them (in vain).

Children's failure to adequately distinguish between fantasy and reality can affect their likes and dislikes regarding media productions in important ways. First, because fantasy and cartoon characters are perceived as real, they can be just as attractive and engaging as real-life characters. By the time they are 3 years old, children start to make statements indicating identification with television characters (Jaglom & Gardner, 1981). But because they can not distinguish between fantasy and reality, they can just as easily focus their attachment on an animal or a fantasy character as on a real-life character. Another implication of children's limited understanding of fantasy and reality is that some special effects or stunts, such as a character vanishing in a puff of smoke, can have a great impact on preoperational children. Because they can not put these events into perspective by understanding that they are cinematic tricks, young children may be more strongly affected by them.

The research discussed earlier suggests that by the time children are 3 or 4 years old, they are reasonably capable of understanding their own fantasies. This means that when playing out fantasy stories, they can remind themselves that their actions are "just pretend." However, it is not until the age of 7 that children are able to deploy their knowledge about fantasy and reality when they watch frightening fiction (Harris, 2000). From the age of 6, children can be prompted to think that something they see or imagine is not real. From then onward, one can effectively say to a child: "This is not real." When children are about 7, they are progressively able to use information about the reality status of a media production autonomously and deliberately when they watch a frightening fictional media production.

Perceptual Boundedness and Centration

One of the most characteristic qualities of preschoolers' thinking is their tendency to focus their attention on the immediately perceptible attributes of an object, image, or product, whereas other types of information that are less obvious or less visually prominent are ignored. This characteristic is sometimes referred to as *perceptual boundedness* (Bruner, 1966). Research shows, for example, that in evaluating characters, preschoolers weigh a character's appearance more heavily than his or her behavior or motivations. In an experiment by Hoffner and Cantor (1985), different groups of children watched a film with a female protagonist. The protagonist's appearance (attractive vs. ugly) and behavior (kind vs. cruel) were manipulated. Preschool children were more inclined than older children to say that the ugly character was cruel and the attractive character was kind, independently of how she had behaved. Older children's responses, on the other hand, were primarily influenced by the protagonist's behavior rather than her appearance.

Closely related to perceptual boundedness is *centration*, the tendency to center attention on an individual, striking feature of an object, image, or product, to the exclusion of other less striking features (Piaget, 1954). An illustrative example of this tendency of young children is a qualitative study reported in Acuff (1997). In this study, 5- to 8-year-old girls were presented with three dolls. Two of the dolls were very expensive, had beautiful, realistic faces and sophisticated mechanical effects. The third doll was much more cheaply made, but had a big red sequined heart on her dress. To the surprise of the researchers, the majority of the girls preferred the cheap doll with the sequined heart. This type of behavior is characteristic of toddlers and preschoolers. They focus their attention on one striking feature, demonstrating that they still have little eye for multiple details. It should be noted, however, that centration occurs primarily when children are confronted with a stimulus for the first time. With repeated exposure, they seem better able to pay attention to multiple details. This might explain why young children often like to watch a media production more than once: It is only after watching it repeatedly that they can grasp the whole content of the production.

Perceptual boundedness and centration have important implications for children's preferences regarding media productions. Until they are approximately 5 years old, children are very visual in their orientation to the world and certainly to media characters. Their descriptions of television characters tend to fix on single, physical attributes without integrating them into an overall picture. They pay less attention to what characters are doing or saying, and pay most attention to simple, brightly colored visuals and colorful, friendly, uncomplicated characters, such as *Teletubbies* and *Barney and Friends* (Jaglom & Gardner, 1981).

EARLY ELEMENTARY SCHOOL (AGE 5–8): ADVENTURE AND REMOTE CONTEXTS

Many of the characteristics of preschoolers also apply to early-elementary school children. Most children between the ages of 5 and 8 still exhibit the characteristic of perceptual boundedness and centration, although these tendencies are clearly on the decline. Children's ability to distinguish fantasy and reality is also in transition. Almost all children in this age group know that Big Bird from *Sesame Street* is a person dressed in a costume. They also appreciate that unrealistic stunts and special effects on television are unreal. However, they still consider something that looks real on television as real, even if it is not (Wright, Huston, Reitz, & Piemyat, 1994). For example, they think that actors on television have their televised professions in real life, and they think that the families in television sitcoms (e.g., as the Huxtables in the *Cosby Show*) are real families. This latter belief is also still common among many 9- and 10-year-olds (Howard, 1998).

There are, however, a number of changes in early elementary school children that justify segmenting them as a separate age group. First, the attention span of children in this age group becomes considerably larger. Whereas 3-year-olds are able to concentrate on a single task for an average of only 18 minutes—and are easily distracted during this time—many 5-year-olds are able to work on a task or computer game for more than an hour (Anderson et al., 1986; Ruff & Lawson, 1990). Second, the development of imaginative play reaches a peak between the ages of 5 and 8 (Fein, 1981). By the age of 4, children's fantasy play becomes more social and they increasingly play with peers. In addition, their fantasy play develops from loose fragments into complex plots. Unlike toddlers and young preschoolers, children in this age group prefer more adventurous themes in their play, such as locations in foreign countries or in outer space.

Loss of Interest in Educational Preschool Programs

By the time they are 5, children's interest in educational preschool programs such as *Sesame Street* starts to decline (Rice, Huston, Truglio, & Wright, 1990).

Children now develop a preference for more fast-paced and complex entertainment with less friendly characters. They prefer to watch more "dangerous" media productions with somewhat more complicated characters, and more remote, adventurous contexts. They also develop an interest in simple forms of verbal humor, such as playing with the sound of words or the incongruous labeling of objects and events—and start to appreciate humor based on conceptual incongruity, such as the exaggeration or distortion of familiar concepts and situations (McGhee, 1979). Finally, they begin to appreciate more malicious and socially unacceptable types of humor. Humor involving human excrement can make many preschoolers howl with laughter.

In our observation study into the attention of toddlers and preschoolers, discussed earlier, we investigated which scenes especially attract the attention of 4- to 5-year-olds. We also aimed to develop a list of the most appealing scenes for children of this age. To our surprise, such a list was difficult to produce because the large majority of the children paid nearly constant attention to the 40-minute videotape. More specifically, all the children had their eyes on the screen during 77% of the scenes. This result agrees with the observation study of Anderson and colleagues (1986), which shows that children of this age pay attention to the screen nearly 70% of the time that the television is turned on.

Our study showed some marked differences between the media preferences of the toddlers and those of the 4- to 5-year-olds. First, hardly any of the *Teletubbies* scenes were among the most appealing scenes among the 4- to 5-year-olds. The only *Teletubbies* scene that did attract the attention of the 4- to 5-year-olds was one in which a Tubbie Toast suddenly jumped into the air. However, such sudden surprises always attract the attention of viewers, irrespective of their age. Such scenes call on the *orienting reflex* of humans. When persons of any age are confronted with a flash of light, a sudden movement, or a loud noise, they orient their attention to it, even before they identify what it is. Research has demonstrated that children and adults do not differ regarding the stimuli that *grab* their attention, but that they do differ as to the stimuli that *hold* their attention (Cohen, 1972; Siegler, 1998).

The scenes that drew a lot of attention among the 4- to 5-year-olds were in part consistent with those that attracted the attention of toddlers. For example, applause, cheering, dancing, singing, and music remained popular among the older preschoolers. An important difference compared to the infants and toddlers, however, was that the older children had a better eye for the content and story line of the program segments. The 4- to 5-year-olds were curious to see what happened next in the stories. Suspenseful contents—such as playing hide and seek in *Sesame Street* and a chase in *Lion King II*—also drew their attention. Such media content apparently is in agreement with the preferences and play themes of children in this age group, in which suspense and adventure plays an important role.

Attraction to Adventure, Action, and Violence

Children in the ages of 5 to 8, especially boys, sometimes develop a strong prefer-ence for entertainment programs with little educational value—often to the great annoyance of their parents. The preference of children is clearly illustrated by the series of universally favorite entertainment programs for this age group that have been released since the 1980s, such as the *Teenage Mutant Ninja Turtles*, *Power Rangers*, and *Pokémon*. This type of children's entertainment, which usu-ally causes media hypes on a world-wide scale, has a number of standard charac-teristics, namely action, violence, binary characters (good–evil, male–female), and narrative simplism (Seiter, 1998).

How can this type of entertainment, which is often systematically rejected by adults, have such a tremendous appeal to children in this age group? Several explanations are available. First, these programs offer an abundance of objects and images that children like, such as action, physical humor, and animated toys. According to some authors, the action and violence of these programs en-dorse rebellion against the restrictions adults impose on their children. The fast-paced action of the superheroes in these entertainment programs offers children the opportunity to escape from their everyday limitations. This is why they speak so much to children in this age group, who themselves are just ex-ploring and experimenting with their physical limits. Through identification with the superheroes in these series, children are able to fantasize that they are strong and powerful, and the feelings that accompany these fantasies provide them with great pleasure.

A second characteristic these programs have in common is that the story usually evolves in a community of peers and friends, which makes them extra appealing to children of this age, who are very interested in social play and in-teractions with peers. Another thing is that the stories and characters in these programs are presented in terms of binary contradictions (Davies, Buckingham, & Kelley, 2000; Seiter, 1998). The characters are, for example, good or evil, or either extremely male or extremely female. Children of this age group, and many older children as well, like to watch these types of simple sto-ries and characters that present the world in terms of simple contradictions, in ways that adults would reject as too stereotypical. Children in this age group are busy with the development of their social identity in general and their gender role identity in particular. They might use the stereotypical characters that ap-pear in these entertainment programs to enable this developmental process (Davies et al., 2000; Seiter, 1998).

In conclusion, this type of entertainment seems to have a number of func-tions for children. The fact that children, especially boys, from all over the world choose to watch this type of entertainment is reason to assume that it sat-isfies some of their needs, such as those for action, identification with powerful superheroes, and information about gender roles and moral norms. It is also obvious that this type of entertainment teaches children some knowledge and skills, although these are not necessarily the knowledge and skills adults would opt for (Seiter, 1998).

These children's entertainment programs are rejected by parents not only because of the low educational value, but often also because of the high doses of violence they contain. Young children, and boys in particular, can feel irresistibly attracted to the violence in these programs. This can be difficult for parents, because boys who are attracted to this type of program can become restless and aggressive in their play (see chap. 3, this volume). In contemporary families, it is inevitable that the media will occasionally confront children with norms, values, and role models that are in disagreement with those of their parents. Forbidding these programs is often not a suitable remedy because this type of entertainment is ubiquitous. Sophisticated marketing strategies enable each newly produced media entertainment project to permeate the farthest corners of children's culture, including television programs, computers, commercials, playgrounds, and toy stores. Parents, teachers, and policy makers should, therefore, realize that the media offer children a pedagogy that cannot do without a counter pedagogy. In the next chapter, I discuss some strategies to modify or counteract undesirable media effects on children.

LATER ELEMENTARY SCHOOL (AGE 8–12): REALISM, CONFORMITY AND FASTIDIOUSNESS

In contrast to younger children, who often focus their attention to one striking characteristic of a stimulus, children in this age group are able to decenter. When 8- to 12-year-olds are confronted with a new stimulus, each characteristic and detail of it is carefully observed. For example, when children of this age get new sports shoes, each part of the shoe, from the laces to the brand logo, is scrutinized carefully and evaluated critically. Children now also become more skeptical about commercials and entertainment programs of low quality, such as those that are repetitious or poorly produced. They are no longer impressed by special effects and fantasy creatures with supernatural powers, and they seem to agree that such elements by themselves are not sufficient to make an entertainment program attractive (Gunter, McAleer, & Clifford, 1991).

Their emergent eye for detail explains why some children in this age group develop a preference for collecting objects, such as dolls or trading cards bearing images of their heroes. Whereas many younger children also tend to collect, their collecting is usually more a matter of "accumulating" (Acuff, 1997, p. 92). Older children, however, often collect with the aim of making distinctions between the different objects, and sometimes also for the social opportunities that collecting offers, such as exchanging objects and playing games.

The Ability to Understand the Difference Between Fantasy and Reality

Throughout elementary school, children are increasingly able to distinguish the real from the unreal in media productions. The fantasies of 8- to 12-year-olds often entail plausible themes. In this period, children become interested in real-world phenomena and seek to discover reality in media productions (Mielke, 1983). Children can be very critical of entertainment and commercials that lack realism, for instance, when actors behave in an unlikely manner, or products are presented in a fantasy context (Gunter et al., 1991).

Although children in this age group start to seek information about the real world, they still appreciate dramatic conflict, rapid action, and comic escapism. Especially, boys up to the age of 12 remain interested in fantastic action-adventure shows, in which the good guys take a stand against the bad guys. Like toddlers and preschoolers, children in this age group still like animals but are now mainly interested in real animals. Because most fantasy characters have been demystified, children in this age group tend to identify with realistic human heroes, such as film stars, sports heroes, and realistic action heroes (Sheldon, 1998).

Sociocognitive Development and Entertainment Preferences

So far I have only discussed the impact of children's cognitive development on their preferences regarding entertainment and media productions. However, children are also social beings who strive to understand their social environment. From the age of 7 and older, children become progressively social. It is plausible that especially at this age a child's sociocognitive level starts to codetermine his or her preferences for media productions. Social cognition includes recognizing and dealing with the emotions of others and understanding social relations and customs (Flavell, Miller, & Miller, 1993). In the following sections, I describe how a child's social-cognitive level affects his or her preferences regarding media productions.

Understanding Emotions

An important characteristic of children aged between 8 and 12 is that they are more capable than younger children of recognizing and understanding the emotions of others. By the time they are 4 or 5, children can explain why their playmates are happy, angry, or sad but tend to rely primarily on visible cues, such as facial expressions (Flavell et al., 1993). From around the age of 6 or 7, children progressively tend to rely on both internal and external cues to interpret emotions. They also start to understand that someone can experience more than one emotion at the same time and that emotions can be feigned (Flavell et al., 1993). This is why children at this level of sociocognitive development start to recognize and dislike poor acting by protagonists in entertainment programs, for example, when actors in soap operas or sitcoms display emotions in an unconvincing way (Gunter et al., 1991; Sheldon & Loncar, 1996).

Understanding Social Perspectives

Children's ability to see the world from another's perspective steadily increases during their years at elementary school (Flavell et al., 1993). According to Piaget (1929), children up to the age of 6 are egocentric in their thinking. By this, Piaget did not mean to say that young children are selfish, but that they are not yet able to think from the social perspectives (thoughts, emotions) of others. Piaget chose the term *egocentrism* to explain some aspects of the child's language. In their early years, children often talk without any intention of communicating. They repeat what they have just heard or simply talk to themselves. Piaget named such talk egocentric.

During early and middle childhood, children gradually develop from mainly egocentric beings (roughly 3 years old) into advanced role takers (roughly 12 to 15). Although preschoolers are somewhat capable of putting themselves in another person's shoes, it is only when children reach elementary school age that they learn to simultaneously consider different points of view and to anticipate and understand how others will react in different situations. The development of such role-taking skills has important consequences for children's understanding of human relationships. For example, whereas preschoolers often think that any pleasant interaction with available playmates qualifies these playmates as friends, from 8 years on, children start to appreciate that their interests and those of their peers can be similar, but also different. At this time, they start to look for friends who are psychologically similar to themselves (Selman, 1980).

Children's growing role-taking ability affects not only the way in which they deal with real-life persons but also the way in which they perceive media characters. Research has shown that children in middle childhood begin to enjoy watching media characters who seem psychologically similar to them. Whereas preschoolers tend to rely on physical similarities between themselves and media characters, older children rely more on psychological and social similarities between their own and a character's personality (Fernie, 1981; Hoffner & Cantor, 1991). For example, in middle childhood it is relatively important whether a character has a good sense of humor or a striking way of making eyes at girls.

Children in middle childhood may have a strong preference for adult characters who make a fool of themselves or behave in a childish way. This type of character commonly appears in certain types of sitcoms (e.g., *Friends*) or animation series aimed at adults (e.g., *The Simpsons* and *Beavis and Butt-head*). Characteristic of these characters is that they combine autonomy and freedom (e.g., living in your own apartment with your friends) with childish aspects, such as irresponsibility, disobedience, and disrespect. By doing so, they offer children the opportunity to prepare for and experiment with a future adult identity, without completely losing the advantages of childhood. Finally, children of this age have a special preference for entertainment in which adults with authority, such as teachers and police officers, suffer a defeat (Davies et al., 2000; Kellner, 1998).

Watching characters who resemble them in physical or psychological respect offers children the opportunity to observe situations and events that may be relevant to their own lives. It stands to reason, therefore, that children pay more attention to the actions of same-gender characters and dislike watching characters who are younger than themselves. Eight- to twelve-year-olds prefer to watch actors of at least their own age, but preferably teenagers or adults. In a study by Sheldon and Loncar (1996) that had children explain why they prefer to see adults, children indicated that adults were involved in more interesting and exciting activities and were better actors.

Enjoyment of media productions is not always predicted by perceived similarity to a character (Hoffner & Cantor, 1991). Heroes like *Harry Potter* and such larger-than-life characters as *Superman* are undoubtedly dissimilar to most child viewers. Still, children are very much attracted to media productions featuring characters like these. Rather than feeling similar, children see these characters as individuals to emulate. Children enjoy vicariously participating in the behaviors of someone they admire and would like to resemble but whom they do not have the capacity to imitate. Wishful identification with admirable characters can help children feel more powerful at a time when they are struggling with real-life problems that are not instantaneously resolvable.

Conformity and the Role of Peers

Peer interactions become increasingly sophisticated among school-aged children. A peer group in middle childhood is a stable confederation of children who share common interests and explicit norms that dictate how members should behave. Because children in this age group develop such a strong sense of commitment and loyalty to the norms of their peer group, they are increasingly sensitive to the thoughts, opinions, judgments, and evaluations of other children. They become very sensitive about how to behave and form strong social antennas for the trends of the moment. They therefore become alert to how to behave in public and how to avoid being ridiculed with respect to what they wear or prefer to watch on television.

For some children, this sensitivity to the opinions of peers starts before they are 6, but it commonly reaches a peak between 11 and 13 years of age (Constanzo & Shaw, 1966). By the time they are 8, children may have developed a strong aversion to programs designed for younger children. Especially in a group context, they may reject shows that feature characters younger than they are. Conversely, it can be considered fashionable in older age groups to watch entertainment programs made for preschoolers. An illustrative example is the *Teletubbies*. This series, which was aimed at toddlers, became a rage among certain adolescent subcultures. This striking phenomenon shows how easily and dramatically a child's individual taste for entertainment can be overruled by the norms of the peer group to which he or she belongs.

Preferences of Entertainment Designed for Adults: Tweenagers

By the time children are 9 years old, they are mainly interested in entertainment designed for adults. In a study by Rosengren and Windahl (1989), 87% of the boys and 80% of the girls in third grade had an adult program as their main preference. Children say that one of the reasons they watch such programs is to be taught social lessons, such as how to behave in relationships. They also watch entertainment designed for adults, especially soaps, to get information about how to deal with personal problems. According to Luke (1990), children feel attracted to these programs because they are made with higher budgets and more sophisticated production techniques.

By the time they are nine or ten, children start to lose interest in toys and become especially interested in products with a social function, such as clothing, music, and sports equipment (Buijzen & Valkenburg, 2000a). These changes have become so obvious in the past years that the 9 to 12 age group has been discovered and segmented as separate niche market by market researchers: the tweenagers. As discussed in the previous chapter, tweenagers often exhibit the preferences and the consumer behavior that used to be common among older adolescents. In some of our studies, we have also observed that the media uses and preferences of 9- to 12-year-olds are in many ways similar to those of adolescents. For example, in our study into children's positive and negative experiences with the Internet, some of the 9- to 12-year-olds used the Internet in ways similar to those of adolescents. For example, they—like adolescents—were interested in Web sites that offer the opportunity for social interaction in the spheres of sex, romance, and dating (Valkenburg & Soeters, 2001).

DIFFERENCES BETWEEN THE MEDIA PREFERENCES OF BOYS AND THOSE OF GIRLS

Although today's girls are different from girls of earlier generations, important and meaningful differences have been found in the way boys and girls typically think, how they express themselves, and what they value. How do differences between the preferences of boys and those of girls arise? Are boys and girls born with an inclination to develop different preferences, or are these gender differences the result of different socialization processes? Many researchers have observed that in the first 18 to 24 months, there does not appear to be any significant gender difference in play style and toy preference (Fagot, 1994). Boys and girls enjoy playing with dolls, cars, and trucks to the same degree, and do not seem to differ in their liking for TV characters, such as *Barney, Big Bird*, and the *Teletubbies*, or in their liking of computer games designed for toddlers (Goldstein, 1998).

However, this gender-neutral preference for toys and entertainment changes rapidly. Significant gender differences in toy preference have been observed as early as 14 months, and by the time children are 3 years old, gender differences are prominent and consistently observable. At this age, boys and girls frequently participate in different activities, avoid toys that are perceived to belong to the opposite sex and play primarily in same-sex groups. This process of gender segregation is found in a variety of cultures and settings (Leaper, 1994; Maccoby, 1988, 1990).

Why is it that for the first 18 months of their lives boys and girls act in a gender-neutral way and then undergo such a dramatic change? There is as yet no consensus about the answer to this question. The emerging gender differences are often attributed to differences in the socialization of boys and girls. From the moment children are born, parents have different expectations of boys and girls, and these are expressed in their communication with their child. Parents talk differently to boys and girls, they are dressed differently, and they receive different toys (O'Brien & Huston, 1985).

Another factor that is believed to contribute to the development of gender segregation is *behavioral compatibility*. This is the phenomenon that boys and girls, at the age of 2 or 3, start to develop distinct interests, which are not shared by their opposite-sex peers. As a result, boys start to like playing with boys and girls with girls (Martin, 1994). It has repeatedly been found that boys engage in more physically aggressive forms of play, such as pretend fights and conquests, and sports such as football. Girls' play, on the other hand, often involves fine motor skills, such as dressing dolls, making jewelry, and other crafts. In the segregated boys' and girls' playgroups that emerge at age 3, different norms for social interaction prevail, and it is assumed that these norms have a powerful influence on the further socialization of boys and girls (Goldstein, 1998; James & McCain, 1982; Leaper, 1994; Maccoby, 1988, 1990).

Gender Differences in Early Childhood

The emerging differences between boys and girls are clearly reflected in their preferences for media productions. In comparison to preschool girls, preschool boys have a strong preference for action and violence in storybooks and entertainment programs. They tend to prefer such themes as sports, fantasy violence, and dangerous scenarios, involving, for example, dinosaurs and aliens. They are attracted to heroic male characters with supernatural powers (e.g., the *Power Rangers* or *Hercules*) and to sports celebrities, knights, soldiers, doctors, and police officers.

Preschool girls are more interested in relationship-centered and nurturing themes. They prefer themes and contexts such as castles, dance studios, schools, circuses, and farmyards, and prefer to focus on such characters as fashion models, ballerinas, good fairies, and princesses. Research has shown that boys mainly identify with male characters, whereas girls can become attached to characters of both sexes. Girls' relatively frequent attraction to male characters probably results from the fact that there are more male characters in the media, who generally also have more exciting and interesting roles than female characters (Hoffner & Cantor, 1991).

Gender Differences in Middle Childhood

During the elementary school years, the preferences of boys and girls for media productions continue to diverge. In particular by the age of 6, most children appear to hold rigid and mutually exclusive sets of beliefs about what the sexes can or cannot do (Ullian, 1977). Because children become increasingly involved with their peers, there is greater pressure to conform to "gender-appropriate" behavior—which is why the differences between the tastes of boys and those of girls become stronger with age. Toy manufacturers and advertisers exploit this knowledge. They know by experience that the most successful toys are gender-specific. "When it comes to toys," goes the adage in the toy industry, "girls will be girls and boys will be boys."

Elementary school boys still have a comparatively strong preference for action-oriented and violent programs. They have in general a stronger preference for sport, science fiction, action and adventure, and a greater preference for cartoons. Boys of this age are still strongly attached to male action heroes and power figures, although the heroes are now more realistic (e.g., Arnold Schwarzenegger and Bruce Willis).

Elementary school girls are in general more likely to react negatively to program scenarios involving action, violence, horror, or swearing. In one of our studies, which had children list the characteristics of an entertainment program they would produce if they were an assistant producer, only the girls spontaneously referred to the absence of sex, violence, or coarse language in such a program (Valkenburg & Janssen, 1999).

Research on girls' preferences for computer games suggests that girls are generally less object-oriented than boys. They are less interested than boys in devices, such as futuristic weapons. For girls, it is not so much about winning or killing the enemy. Girls like a story line. They, more often than boys, like to watch realistic drama that focuses on the development of relationships between real-life characters. Elementary school girls prefer family situations, and enjoy serial dramas with realistic themes. They are most interested in realistic, attractive characters, such as models, film stars, and male and female sports and music celebrities. They are more interested than boys in dramatic story lines, and attach more value to the comprehensibility of an entertainment program. Teenage females are more eager than teenage males to look for actors or actresses they recognize. They invest more time in searching for information about shows and characters, and prefer to watch an entertainment show from start to finish (Heeter, 1988; Sanger, Willson, Davis, & Whittaker, 1997; Valkenburg & Janssen, 1999).

The scarce research on gender differences regarding preferences for romance in media productions has yielded mixed results. Girls are probably more likely to watch romantic themes if the focus is on love and the development of relationships. Boys may prefer romance if sexuality and its taboo nature is the focus (Valkenburg & Cantor, 2000). A study by De Bruin (1999) suggests, however, that the differences between teenage males and females regarding preferences for romance have become less evident in the past decade. On the basis of his content analysis of various British and Dutch magazines for the young, such as *Sugar, Break Out,* and *Top of the Pops,* de Bruin argued that the *romantic perspective,* in which a female waits until a male fancies her, has progressively become less prominent in magazines for the young since the early 1990s. The so-called *macho perspective* seems to be gaining strength, however: Female adolescents increasingly adopt the language that is traditionally used by boys, and increasingly take the initiative when it comes to sex. However, it is still an open question whether these developments indicate the disappearance of gender differences in the perception of romance in media productions.

Conclusion

A literature review on gender differences in media preferences runs the risk of confirming or even reinforcing traditional gender-role stereotypes. In the preceding sections, I reviewed some general trends in the differences in the media preferences of boys and girls; however, it is important to realize that male and female children and adolescents are often more heterogeneous than researchers presume. For example, it is not the case that only girls are interested in media productions in which the development of relationships between characters is the focus. If it were the case, the immense popularity of the *Dungeons and Dragons* computer games among males would be inexplicable because in these games the development of relationships between characters is the pre-eminent focus.

In this chapter, I have discussed a number of differences in the media preferences between younger and older children and between males and females. Although these differences have been found in various studies, the conclusions have usually been based on aggregated data, in that results of different subgroups of children have been compared. It is important, however, to keep in mind that children within an age or gender group can sometimes vary as much as children in different age groups.

3

Media Violence and Aggression

Of all issues related to children and the media, the influence of violent entertainment on aggressive behavior has undoubtedly received most research attention. This chapter provides insight into the current state of the empirical research on this topic. Consisting of four sections, the first discusses the different types of effect studies that have been conducted, identifying their strong and weak points. The second section reviews the various theories that attempt to explain why media violence may effect aggressive behavior, such as the social learning theory, cognitive script theory, arousal theory, and desensitization theory. The third section focuses on differentiations in the effects of media violence, such as the characteristics in media productions that stimulate or reduce aggressive behavior, and the factors influencing children's susceptibility to media violence. The final section concentrates on how adults can modify or counteract possible adverse effects of media violence on children.

FIVE TYPES OF RESEARCH ON THE EFFECTS OF MEDIA VIOLENCE

Public concern about the effects of media violence on aggressive behavior existed long before television was introduced. However, the empirical research that investigates whether there is a basis for this concern did not burgeon until the 1960s, when growing fear about increasing delinquency in American inner cities developed. Since then, numerous studies have been conducted into the impact of media violence on the aggressive behavior of children and young people.

To understand and critically evaluate the research into the impact of media violence on aggressive behavior, it is necessary to overview the nature of the research that has been conducted. The empirical research into the impact of media violence can be classified into five types of studies: (1) laboratory experiments, (2) field experiments, (3) correlational studies, (4) causal-correlational studies, and (5) meta-analyses. I start this chapter with a discussion of each of these types of research.

Laboratory Experiments

In a laboratory experiment, a group of children is invited to come to a laboratory, usually consisting of one or more rooms, in which sound and video equipment is installed. In a typical laboratory experiment, one half of the children are assigned to view a violent film (the experimental group), and the other half to a neutral film or no film at all (the control group). After the films, the investigators measure whether the children who have been exposed to the violent film are more aggressive than those in the control group. The majority of the laboratory experiments have found that children who are exposed to violent films exhibit higher levels of postviewing aggression than do children assigned to the control group. These children played more aggressively, behaved more aggressively toward peers, or hit dolls or toys harder (Wood, Wong, & Chachere, 1991).

An important characteristic of the laboratory experiment is that children are randomly assigned to either the experimental or the control group; thus, each subject in the experiment has an equal probability of being assigned to the experimental or the control group. Random assignment minimizes the likelihood that differences between the experimental and control group are due to initial differences among the children, rather than to true experimental effects. Laboratory experiments, therefore, have a high internal validity, which implies that researchers finding an increase in aggression among children in the experimental group can be quite confident that this increase is the result of the children's exposure to the violent film. In other words, there are no serious competing explanations for children's increased postviewing aggression scores.

Although the internal validity of laboratory experiments is high, this type of research does have its limitations. One of the most important drawbacks is that these experiments usually take place in an artificial setting. Laboratory experiments, therefore, typically lack external validity, which refers to the extent to which the results of a study can be generalized to children's everyday life. As a result, researchers can not guarantee that their results will hold true in children's everyday life. This weakness of laboratory experiments has often been criticized by cultural studies researchers, who believe that experimental research pays too little attention to the social context within which children's exposure to violence occurs.

Field Experiments

The lack of external validity does not hold for field experiments, which are usually conducted in children's natural environment. In field experiments, also referred to as quasi-experiments (Cook & Campbell, 1979), researchers investigate existing groups in such settings as schools or children's homes. As a result, they often are not able to control all the circumstances of their study. In field experiments, children are typically exposed to either a violent or a nonviolent television diet for several days or weeks. One example of a classic field experiment is a Belgium study by Leyens, Camino, Park, and Berkowitz (1975), in which a group of children from an institution for problem children watched violent films each evening for a week, while another group watched neutral films. The children who had seen the violent films were subsequently more aggressive than the children who had seen the neutral films. The effect of the films held particularly for the children who were initially more aggressive.

Another type of field experiment is the natural experiment. A well-known natural experiment was published in Canada in the 1980s. In this study by Joy, Kimball, and Zabrack (1986), the researchers compared the aggressive behavior of children who lived in a town without television—Notel—to that of children from two towns with television. The children in the three towns were reinvestigated 2 years later, by which time Notel had obtained television. The children in Notel had become more aggressive following the introduction of television in their town, whereas the level of aggression of the children in the other two towns had remained the same.

Field experiments have an advantage over laboratory experiments in that they are conducted in children's natural environment. This type of research, therefore, has a comparatively high external validity. An important drawback of field experiments, however, is that researchers can not be sure that factors other than the experimental treatment have caused the change in behavior. Although researchers can control for certain variables that they suspect to codetermine the relation between media violence and aggression (e.g., intelligence and socioeconomic status), they are not able to recognize and exclude all possible third variables. Thus, field experiments have a comparatively low internal validity; that is, researchers are not able to attribute their results with certainty to the violent films. Therefore, researchers are not able to draw definitive conclusions based on their field experiments. At best, they can conclude that their findings are plausible.

Correlational Studies

Like field experiments, correlational studies are conducted in children's natural environment. Correlational studies are based on the assumption that if media violence stimulates aggression, children who watch lots of media violence should be more aggressive than children who are less avid consumers of media violence. In other words, if media violence stimulates aggressive behavior, there should be a positive relation between children's viewing frequency and their aggressive behavior.

In correlational studies, researchers usually visit schools or families, armed with a battery of survey questions about the level and types of media violence that children consume. They also measure children's aggression by means of questionnaires, teacher observations, playground observations, or other methods. The majority of correlational studies have demonstrated that the more exposure children have to media violence, the more aggressive they are.

Although correlational studies have an external validity comparable to that of field experiments, they have a lower internal validity. Correlational studies only allow the conclusion that there is a positive relationship between children's viewing frequency and their aggression. Such a relationship does not necessarily mean that children's viewing frequency causes their aggressive behavior. After all, a positive relationship between media violence and aggression could also reflect the reversed causal explanation; that is, that aggressive children are more likely to select violent media in order to satisfy their need for aggressive stimuli. In correlational research, both children's viewing behavior and their aggression are measured at the same point in time. However, in order to demonstrate that media violence causes aggression, and not vice versa, children's viewing of violence must take place before their aggressive behavior. After all, one situation can cause the other only if the first situation takes place before the second and not if these situations occur simultaneously.

Causal-Correlational Studies

This chicken-and-egg problem of correlational research can be solved by means of causal-correlational or longitudinal research. In causal-correlational studies, researchers visit schools or families to measure children's viewing frequency and their aggressive behavior, as in correlational studies. However, they differ from correlational research in that the researchers return to these places after a period of time to re-examine the children. Because children's viewing frequency and their aggressive behavior are assessed at two or more points in time, it is possible to determine whether watching violence causes aggression, or whether aggressive tendencies induce children to select violent media.

A well-known example of a causal-correlational study is the longitudinal study by Huesmann, Moise-Titus, Podolski, and Eron (2003), who surveyed two groups of children twice, once when they were 6 and 8 years old, and then again, 15 years later, when they were 21- and 23-year-olds. At both times, both children's television exposure and their aggressive behavior were measured. The study revealed a significant correlation between watching television violence in childhood and aggressive behavior in adulthood. However, no significant correlation was found between aggressive behavior in childhood and watching television violence in adulthood. Another well-known longitudinal causal-correlational study by Johnson, Smailes, Kasen, and Brook (2002), which was published in the prestigious journal *Science*, found the same pattern of longitudinal relationships between watching violence in childhood and aggressiveness in adulthood. Both of these studies confirm the hypothesis that media violence causes aggressive behavior, and rule out the reverse explanation that aggressive children tend to select violent media.

Meta-Analyses

Meta-analyses are studies in which the results of dozens, or even hundreds, of empirical studies are summarized and re-evaluated by means of sophisticated statistical techniques. In meta-analyses, the statistical data of individual empirical studies are brought together in a new database, which allows the researcher to assess a new effect size by simultaneously analyzing the statistics of the individual empirical studies. The academic community usually respects meta-analyses more than it respects empirical studies, provided that the meta-analysis is conducted carefully and the empirical research included in the analysis is satisfactory. Meta-analyses can lead to sophistications in academic theories, demonstrate which research questions have received more or less attention, and give direction to future empirical research.

Among the meta-analyses conducted since the early 1990s on the impact of media violence on aggressive behavior, two focused on film and television violence, and two on video and computer game violence. Each meta-analysis demonstrated that exposure to media violence results in an increase in violent behavior (Anderson & Bushman, 2001; Paik & Comstock, 1994; Sherry, 2001; Wood et al., 1991). The largest meta-analysis, which included 217 empirical studies, revealed a significant correlation of $r = 0.31$ between watching media violence and aggressive behavior (Paik & Comstock, 1994). A correlation of this size is usually identified as a moderate effect size (Cohen, 1988). As the qualification of a moderate effect size may not be clear to all readers, I explain what such a correlation coefficient means, using a conversion method developed by Rosenthal and Rubin (1982).

According to this conversion method, a correlation of $r = 0.31$ means that there is a 65.5% chance that children whose exposure to media violence is higher than the median[1] will display aggressive behavior, while there is a 34.5% chance that children who are exposed to media violence below the median will display such behavior. This 31% difference in the likelihood of displaying aggressive behavior between children who are exposed to media violence either above or below the median has great practical importance (Bushman & Huesmann, 2001; McCartney & Rosenthal, 2000).

THEORIES ON THE INFLUENCE OF MEDIA VIOLENCE ON AGGRESSIVE BEHAVIOR

Although the meta-analyses have demonstrated that media violence can lead to aggressive behavior, an equally important question is how this occurs. In the literature, a number of theories prevail. Each of these theories offers an explanation why media violence can cause aggressive behavior.

Social Learning Theory

According to the social learning theory (Bandura, 1986, 1994), aggression is a form of conduct learned in the same way that other human conduct is learned. First, children learn to act aggressively by direct experience. During interactions with their social environment, some actions prove successful, others evoke no perceptible effects, and still others produce negative consequences. Based on this feedback, children tend to select the successful actions and to discard the unsuccessful ones. Young children test their environment to find out which behavior is considered desirable and which is not. Hammering fiercely in the shed is allowed, but smashing into the furniture is not tolerated by most parents. Parents' approving and disapproving responses teach the child which behaviors are socially regarded as right and which are not. When aggressive acts are punished, children learn to control and censure their conduct and impulses. However, if children experience that their aggressive acts are successful, they will more regularly use violence to reach their goal, until violence has become a routine that cannot easily be changed (Bandura, 1973, 1986).

Aggressive behavior can also be learned by observing the consequences of violent acts performed by other people. With this type of learning, children do not directly experience rewards or punishments but become aware of them through the models in their environment. When children see that the actions of

---

[1]The median is the middle score in a series of scores; that is, exactly 50% of the scores fall above or below this point (e.g., 9 is the median in the following series of numbers: 3, 4, 9, 12, 15). To read more about this conversion method, called the Binomial Effect Size Display (BESD), see Rosenthal and Rubin (1982), and McCartney and Rosenthal (2000).

others produce unpleasant outcomes, the likelihood that they will behave in a similar way decreases. For example, if a child observes that his or her older brother kicks the dog and is consequently reprimanded by their father, the younger child will vicariously experience that it is wrong to kick dogs. Conversely, if children experience that the actions of others are successful, the likelihood that they will adopt this behavior increases. A child who observes that his older brother kicks the dog in the presence of several friends, and that these friends express amusement about the howling dog, may pick up a quite different standard of behavior. It is not difficult to predict which of these two children will later kick his or her dog.

Learning aggressive behavior thus takes place not only by direct experience with the positive and negative consequences of certain behavior but also by learning how models in the children's environment fare with a specific conduct. This second form of learning—observational learning—is especially likely to occur when the model's actions are successful, when the model is attractive, and when children reside in communities in which aggressive models are plentiful. Bandura (1973) identified three important sources of aggressive models: the family, the subculture within which a child lives, and the mass media.

Bandura tested his theory in several studies. In one of his classic bobo doll experiments, he had a group of preschoolers watch a film in which an adult man hits and kicks an adult-size plastic doll (called *Bobo*). Children were randomly assigned to one of three versions of this film. The first group of children watched a version of the film in which the man was rewarded for his aggressive acts: Another man told him that he was a "strong champion." He receives chocolate bars and a large glass of 7-Up. The second group of children saw the man perform the same actions, but he is now punished; he is spanked with a rolled-up magazine and the second adult tells him: "If I catch you doing that again, you big bully, I'll give you a hard spanking." The third group of children watched a neutral version of the film, in which the man was neither rewarded nor punished for his aggressive acts. After the film, all the children were provided with the opportunity to play with the bobo doll. Those who had seen the film with the rewarded model, imitated more aggressive acts than did the children who had seen the film with the punished or neutral models (Bandura, 1965).

According to Bandura (1986), the influence of violent media characters is not limited to imitation effects. In addition to direct imitation, such as how to hit and kick a bobo doll, media characters also influence children in their opinions and norms about the use of aggression. In fictional media productions, physical aggression often seems to be the only means to resolve interpersonal problems. Physical violence is often portrayed as justified, acceptable, and rewarding. The heroes hesitate as little as the villains to kill and murder, and are usually rewarded amply for their aggressive acts. One of the general lessons that children learn from media characters is that violence works and is an appropriate way to solve interpersonal conflicts.

Bandura's social learning theory is still one of the most widely accepted theories on the impact of media violence. His publications in the 1960s instigated a variety of studies into the factors that codetermine the learning of aggression through observational learning. Researchers started to pay attention to such questions as: Why is one child more susceptible than another? Which environmental factors codetermine the relationship between media violence and aggression? The studies based on Bandura's initial theories and experiments have produced several new insights, and based on these insights, Bandura adjusted his social learning theory. In the latest version of this theory, Bandura put more emphasis on children's self-regulatory processes. He no longer assumed that media violence has uniform effects on children. The impact of media violence depends on the characteristics of the media production, of the child, and of his or her social environment (Bandura, 1986, 1994).

Cognitive Script Theory

To understand the cognitive script theory, one needs to know what a cognitive script is. A script can be defined as the knowledge of the structure and order in which routine activities typically occur. By the age of 3, children have a great number of scripts in their memory; for example, a script that describes how people go out for dinner, how they take a bath, or what happens when someone gets angry. Although the particulars of such events usually vary from occasion to occasion, their basic structure is often the same. For example, when you visit the doctor, you make yourself known to the receptionist, you wait in the waiting room, the doctor, assistant, or receptionist calls your name, and you enter the consulting room. This knowledge of the basic structure of activities and events is called a script (Siegler, 1998).

Cognitive scripts are formed by events in the daily lives of children but can also be shaped by media experiences. How can media violence affect the formation of scripts? In media productions, interpersonal problems are often solved by means of aggression: Often, a character who is insulted reciprocates by throwing a punch. If children are frequently exposed to lots of media violence, there is a risk that the scripts in their memory will become more aggressive than those of children who are less avid consumers of media violence. It is assumed that these aggressive, media-induced scripts, which are formed early in childhood, stimulate aggressive attitudes and behavior later in life (Bushman & Huesmann, 2001).

Priming Theory

Just like the cognitive script theory, the priming theory relies heavily on cognitive constructions (i.e., scripts and schemas). This theory is derived from the neo-associative perspective, which considers human memory as a collection of associative networks (Jo & Berkowitz, 1994). Each of these networks consists of many connected units or nodes, which can represent thoughts, emotions, behavioral tendencies, or elements of such. It is assumed that one external stimulus (e.g., a violent film), which activates one or more specific nodes in memory, can simultaneously trigger many other semantically or contiguously related nodes. Not all of these nodes are necessarily related to the original external stimulus. After all, via spreading activation, the observed stimulus can activate a complex series of other nodes (thoughts, feelings, or behavioral tendencies).

According to Berkowitz (1984), media violence can increase the likelihood that certain aggressive nodes become more accessible. This accessibility can be chronic or temporary. When certain aggressive nodes are chronically activated by violent stimuli, the probability that these particular nodes are used continually to understand and interpret media violence is enhanced. However, a violent stimulus can also cause a temporary augmented accessibility of one or more nodes. This temporary accessibility is called priming. In short, priming is the temporary heightened accessibility of nodes that are more or less semantically related to an external stimulus.

The priming theory has been investigated in a study by Bushman (1998). In one of the experiments reported in this study, one half of a group of students was assigned to view a nonviolent videotape, whereas the other half was exposed to *Karate Kid III*. At the end of the films, each participant was presented with 48 words. Half of these words were real English words, the other half were nonexistent words. The participants were told to press one computer key as quickly as possible if they thought the word was an English word, and another one if they thought it was a nonword. However, without the participants' knowledge, half of the words were aggressive and the other half nonaggressive. The students who had seen *Karate Kid III* had faster reaction times than the students who had been exposed to the nonviolent film, but only when it came to the aggressive words. According to Bushman (1998), these faster reactions should be attributed to priming: The violent film caused a temporary heightened accessibility of aggressive nodes in their memory, which in turn caused the faster reaction times.

Arousal Theory

The arousal theory assumes that exposure to media violence arouses children. Arousal is a physical response, which results in increased breathing, heartbeat, blood sugar level, sweat gland activity, and so forth. Media-produced arousal is nonspecific; it can be provoked by violent programs, but also by frightening, suspenseful, and sexually arousing media productions (Zillmann, 1991). When it comes to violent programs, arousal is most likely to be produced when the violence is combined with a lot of action, loud music, and a rapid program pace.

The arousal theory assumes that the media-induced arousal will not immediately fade away after the viewing situation. The physical arousal energizes children's postexposure behavior, which is not steered but intensified. Arousal-inducing media productions may lead to agitation and restlessness, which is expressed in children's play and interactions with other children. The meta-analysis performed by Paik and Comstock (1994) demonstrates that violent media productions that leave children in a state of excitement cause more aggressive behavior than media productions without this quality.

Desensitization Theory

According to this theory, repeated exposure to media violence causes a gradual blunting of emotional responses to displays of aggression, both in the media and in real life. A basic principle in this theory is that the impact of a media stimulus decreases with repeated exposure. Spectators get accustomed to continuous inhumanities: They not only suffer less from them in the end, but also their moral judgments about them seem to become blunted (Frijda, 2001).

Research has shown that this habituation effect can occur after exposure to both mild and more graphic forms of violence. In a study by Linz, Donnerstein, and Penrod (1984), a group of male college students watched, across a 5-day period, a series of films portraying sexual violence against women. After each film, the emotional reactions of the males were measured. The perceptions of and emotional responses to the films changed significantly between the first and the last film. With repeated exposure, the males judged the films as less violent, less offensive, and less degrading to women.

The desensitization hypothesis assumes not only that viewers' reactions to media violence become blunted, but also that these reactions are carried over to their real-life situation. Moreover, it is hypothesized that media-induced desensitization reduces inhibitions against aggression in real life. Negative emotional responses, such as fright or anxiety, have often been shown to operate as restraints against aggressive behavior (Bandura, 1986). Therefore, if children's emotional reactions to violence are reduced or even eliminated, the likelihood that they will engage in aggressive behavior is increased.

Thomas, Horton, Lippincott, and Drabman (1977) investigated how exposure to media violence affects children's reactions to violence in a realistic setting. In this experiment, 40 children aged between 8 and 10 were assigned on an individual basis to view either an episode of a violent police series or a nonviolent volleyball game. Immediately after the film, the experimenter told each child that he was helping a friend who was working with younger children at a nearby location. He continued:

My friend has a TV camera in a playroom in another part of this building. The camera sees and hears everything that goes on in the room. I'm supposed to watch some little kids for my friend now, but I have to make an important phone call. Could you do me a favor and watch them until I get back? I'll only be gone for a few minutes. Here, let me switch the channel so you can see them. Hmmmm, looks like nobody's there right now. They should be there pretty soon. Well anyhow, I'll be right back. Just stay right here and watch the TV while you sit real still. I'll be right back in just a few minutes.

The experimenter had not even left the room when the camera showed a group of preschoolers, who, upon being left alone in the playroom, began to fight with each other. After a while, the fighting children "broke" the camera and it stopped working. While the child watched the video (of course, the camera was a videotape), his or her emotional reaction was measured. The children who had seen the aggressive police film were far less upset by the fighting preschoolers than the children who had been exposed to the nonviolent volleyball game.

Catharsis Theory

Unlike the previous theories, the catharsis theory assumes that watching media violence has a positive influence on children. Advocates of this theory state that violent images can indeed evoke aggressive feelings in children, but that these feelings are purged while watching media violence (Feshbach, 1976). They assume that by nature children have aggressive impulses. By watching aggression in media productions, they get the opportunity to discharge these impulses, and thus behave less aggressively afterward. *Catharsis* means the purification of the emotions by vicarious experience; the concept was first developed by the Greek philosopher, Aristotle, who believed that tragic drama could lead to a release of emotions.

The catharsis theory was especially popular during the early days of television and is still taken seriously in some academic circles (e.g., cultural film and cinema studies). However, the theory has never been confirmed by academic research. Watching media violence may purify children's emotions, but it certainly does not reduce their aggressive behavior. In fact, four meta-analyses and many empirical studies have demonstrated that media violence increases aggressive behavior.

Conclusion

With the exception of the catharsis theory—which assumes that media violence counteracts aggressive behavior, but has never been confirmed—all the theories just discussed offer a plausible explanation for why watching media violence stimulates aggressive behavior. It is not yet clear which theory is most applicable. It is possible that all theories hold more or less for different types of media violence and different types of children.

DIFFERENTIATIONS IN THEORY AND RESEARCH

Modern effect researchers agree that not all types of media violence have the same effect on children. The effects of media violence are moderated by several factors, such as the type of media violence, the child who is watching, and his or her social environment. In the next sections, I discuss some important differentiations in the effects of media violence on aggression.

Different Types of Media Violence

The theory of selective media effects, which has gradually become the leading theory among media-effects researchers, assumes that media violence does have effects, but only under certain conditions. A documentary about the increase of violence among young people, in which violent scenes are portrayed to make the audience aware of this problem in society, of course can not be compared with a slasher film in which the protagonist uses a chainsaw to get rid of his enemies. The documentary is probably meant to discourage violence, whereas in the slasher film the violence is glamorized. It is also not difficult to believe a film such as *Schindler's List* has different effects on viewers than a film like *Terminator II* has (Wilson et al., 1998). Viewers use the context of the media violence to interpret and construct the meaning of the images they view. For media-effects researchers, it is important to investigate how viewers process and interpret the contexts of media violence because media effects are dependent on such interpretations. Research has revealed several context characteristics that moderate the impact of media violence on aggressive behavior. The following are the most important ones.

Identification With the Protagonist. The meta-analysis performed by Paik and Comstock (1994) demonstrates that the effects of media violence are enhanced when protagonists offer the opportunity for identification. When violent media characters are attractive and portrayed in such a way that they increase identification, children are more likely to adopt the aggressive behaviors of these characters. As discussed in the previous chapter, children are mostly attracted to media characters that are similar to them in terms of gender and age. This might be one reason why children are comparatively likely to adopt aggressive behaviors from an aggressive child or teenager (Hicks, 1965).

Rewarded and Punished Violence.   A critical characteristic of violent media productions is whether the aggressive behavior is punished or rewarded. In media productions, children's role models are often the good guys. They are clever, powerful, attractive superheroes, who are rarely punished for their violent acts (Wilson et al., 1998). Several studies have demonstrated that rewarded media violence fosters viewers' acquisition of aggressive attitudes and behavior. In contrast, punished violence can serve to reduce such acquisition (e.g., Bandura, 1965).

Justified and Unjustified Violence.   Suppose that in a film, a father discovers that someone has assaulted and killed his daughter. The father sets out to find the killer and, when he has found him, starts to torture him. The father uses extreme violence in retaliation for the harm the killer has done to someone he loved. Viewers often consider such use of violence justified. Some viewers might even applaud if the father kills his daughter's murderer: "Kill him. It'll serves him right." Conversely, the use of violence by a media character who kills a gas station attendant for not returning his change fast enough, is likely to be considered unjustified. Such violence will not receive much sympathy from viewers (Wilson et al., 1998).

The meta-analysis performed by Paik and Comstock (1994) demonstrates that the likelihood of aggressive behavior is higher when children believe that the protagonist's behavior is justified. An example of a study on the effects of justified media violence is offered by Berkowitz and Powers (1979). In their experiment, male undergraduate students were exposed to a videotape that featured a group of motorcyclists attacking a middle-aged man. Some of the undergraduates were told in advance that the motorcyclists were attacking the man in retaliation for his attack on two fellow motorcyclists, who were seriously hurt (justified violence). The others were told that the motorcyclists belonged to a gang and were attacking the man solely for amusement (unjustified violence). The former group of students behaved more aggressively than the latter group of students.

Children judge justified violence as less wrong than unjustified violence. In one of our studies, we presented children with a story in which somebody was beaten up so seriously that he had to be hospitalized. However, in one version of the story the violence was justified: The perpetrator hit a gang member in defense of his grandmother who was being terrorized by the gang. In the other version, the violence was unjustified: The perpetrator hit someone who had accidentally parked his car too close to the perpetrator's car. As expected, virtually all children (98%) judged the unjustified violence as wrong. However, the justified violence used to protect the grandmother was judged as wrong by only a minority (30%) of the children, whereas 43% of the children judged it as right (Krcmar & Valkenburg, 1999).

Violence Without Harmful Consequences.   Many entertainment productions portray violent interactions without any observable harmful consequences, such as cries of pain, physical injuries, and so forth. This type of unrealistic violence is most common in children's programs and comedies (Wilson et al., 1998). If the violent acts in these programs were to occur in reality, the impact on the victim would be considerably more serious. Gerbner (1992) referred to this type of violence, which omits the painful or tragic consequences for the victims, as happy violence. Exposure to violence with unrealistic harm may stimulate children to develop biased views concerning the consequences of violent acts. They may also develop the belief that real violence has no serious consequences, with the result that constraints on acting aggressively are reduced.

Several studies have demonstrated that children who witness the harmful consequences of media violence subsequently behave less aggressively than children who have not been exposed to these consequences. For example, in an experiment by Wotring and Greenberg (1973), a group of boys who had watched a violent film that showed the victim's injuries were less aggressive than boys who had seen the same film but without these harmful consequences. There are two possible explanations for this finding. First, children who vicariously experience a victim's pain may feel sorry for him or her, and this may inhibit aggressive behavior because empathy with the suffering of others often helps to curb interpersonal aggression. Second, exposure to the harmful consequences of violence may evoke negative emotional responses, such as fright or fear, and again this may inhibit aggressive behavior (Bandura, 1986; Hoffman, 2000).

Realistic Violence.   Several studies have shown that realistic media violence more easily results in aggressive behavior than unrealistic media violence does. Cartoons, for example, generally evoke less strong reactions than films with real-life actors. Media violence also has more impact on viewers if these viewers *think* that it is real. In a study by Berkowitz and Alioto (1973), for example, a televised battle between American and Japanese forces resulted in more aggression when it was presented as a war documentary than when it was presented as a Hollywood film. Realistic violence may encourage violent behavior because realistic perpetrators more easily induce identification in viewers. They may, therefore, serve as a model for children more readily than unrealistic ones do.

Arousing Images.   The meta-analysis performed by Paik and Comstock (1994) demonstrated that arousing media violence encourages aggressive behavior. Arousing violence is often found in American and Japanese children's entertainment series (e.g., *Power Rangers* and *Pokémon*), and in police series. In English and German detective series, arousing violent images are less common (van der Voort, 1997).

Differences Among Children

In the past few decades, effects researchers have developed a better eye for individual differences in children that moderate the effects of media violence on aggressive behavior. The literature details four child factors that have a powerful influence on the media violence–aggression relation: the child's gender, age, and interest in media violence, and the existing attitude toward media violence within the family.

Boys and Girls.   In general, the effects of media violence on aggression are greater for males than for females (Paik & Comstock, 1994). Boys typically have a greater preference for violent action programs, and are more often exposed to such programs—which increases the likelihood that boys will be influenced by these programs. In addition, today's arsenal of popular action and adventure programs (which typically feature male heroes) offers boys more opportunities than girls to identify with aggressive heroes. As identification is an important mediating variable in the media–aggression relation, it is no surprise that boys are more easily affected than girls by media violence.

Younger Children.   Media violence has a greater impact on younger children than on older children. Children younger than six are the most vulnerable. These children typically judge the violence in cartoon and animation programs as just as real as the violence in programs with people made of flesh and blood. As a result, young children are susceptible not only to realistic media violence but also to cartoon and animated violence. For example, young elementary school children can just as easily be physically excited by a cartoon as by a film with real actors. This broader impressionability of young children might be why the largest media effects have been found within the youngest age groups (Paik & Comstock, 1994).

Children Who Have a Special Preference for Media Violence.   Bandura's (1986) social learning theory predicts that children learn violent acts from media characters particularly when they wish to learn these acts. If a young child does not like spinach, it is difficult to persuade him or her to eat spinach. Likewise, if children do not like media violence, they will probably not consume media violence and thus will not be influenced by it. In contrast, if a child strongly identifies with a violent superhero or greatly admires such a hero, the likelihood of aggressive behavior is greatest (Paik & Comstock, 1994).

Children From Violent Families.   The aggression and delinquency of children and teenagers are determined in large part by the level of aggression and delinquency of their parents. Parents who use physical violence to solve problems often have hostile and aggressive children. A violent family environment teaches children the norm that violence works and that violence is okay, because Dad uses it too.

Children from families in which problems are solved by physical violence are more susceptible to the impact of media violence. This is conceivable because for these children, media violence is in agreement with the norms and behavior that prevail in their real-life environment, which can result in resonance effects. However, when children know that violence is rejected and punished in their environment, they may still learn aggressive behavior from media characters, but because the sanctions on aggression are substantial, they will less easily display the aggressive acts they have learned (Bandura, 1986).

ADULT MEDIATION TO MODIFY UNDESIRABLE MEDIA EFFECTS

So far, I have focused on the state of the research into the effects of violent entertainment on aggressive behavior. I have discussed the major theories and provided insight into some widely accepted differentiations in the media-aggression research. In this final section, I discuss another body of literature that is at least as important but not as developed as the effects literature. This literature, which did not burgeon until the 1980s, focuses on the strategies that parents and adults can use to modify or counteract the adverse effects of media violence on children. For today's children, exposure to media violence is virtually inevitable. It is therefore just as necessary to study the effectiveness of strategies to minimize the likelihood of negative media effects, as it is to study the effects of media violence.

The past 2 decades have witnessed an increase in the amount of research on adult mediation of children's media use. Most of this research has focused on the way parents cope with their children's television viewing. Parents have been shown to use three types of television mediation: (a) restrictive mediation (i.e., setting rules concerning or restrictions on exposure); (b) active mediation (i.e., talking to children about television and its content); and (c) coviewing (i.e., adults and children watching television together; Nathanson, 1999; Valkenburg, Valkenburg, Krcmas, Peeters, & Marseille, 1999).

Of these three forms of television mediation, active mediation has been studied most often in the context of mediation outcomes. This research has so far revealed three strategies to modify the effects of violent entertainment. These strategies include a coviewing adult who (a) openly disapproves of the violent acts that are portrayed, (b) emphasizes the fictional nature of the media production, and (c) stimulates children to empathize with the victims. I briefly discuss each of these strategies.

Disapproving Commentary by a Coviewing Adult

Several studies have shown that a coviewing adult who openly disapproves of the filmed violence inhibits subsequent aggression or tolerance for aggression (e.g., Hicks, 1986). In an experiment by Corder-Bolz (1980), for example, 5- to 10-year-old children watched an episode of *Batman* together with a popular teacher. In one experimental condition, the teacher made neutral comments about the *Batman* episode. In another condition, the teacher made disapproving comments, such as "It's bad to fight" and "It's better to get help." The children who watched *Batman* with the disapproving teacher were significantly less accepting of hurting, hitting, and stealing than the children whose viewing was not mediated.

There is also evidence to suggest that the effect of a disapproving adult holds only when the adult coviewer remains present during the postexposure measurement. In a study by Hicks (1986), children between the ages of 5 and 8 were exposed to a short film that featured an adult model who hit a bobo doll. During the film, a male experimenter provided positive statements (e.g., "Boy, look at him go!" and "He sure is a tough guy!"), negative statements (e.g., "That's awful"), or neutral statements. At the end of the film, the children played for 15 minutes with several toys, including the bobo doll shown in the film. One half of the subjects in each of the experimental conditions played with the toys in the presence of the adult coviewer, whereas the other half was unaccompanied. As expected, the children who had heard the negative statements were less likely to imitate the aggressive acts performed by the filmed model. However, this inhibition effect was found only for the children who knew that they were being observed. This suggests that the value of disapproving commentary is limited because it works only in settings in which an adult is present. However, this result is still entirely in agreement with Bandura's (1986) social learning theory, which emphasizes that the performance of aggressive behavior is largely predicted by the child's anticipation of negative consequences. Young children typically rely on the supervision of external socialization agents to keep them out of trouble. Only when they mature do they begin to adopt internal standards of behavior as guides for and restraints on their actions. Because Hicks's study included very young children, it is conceivable that the accompanied (and not the unaccompanied) children were especially susceptible to the disapproving adult.

Pointing Out the Fictional Nature of Entertainment

The adult commentary does not necessarily have to be approving or disapproving. A second strategy to counteract negative media effects is to remind children that a film is not realistic. Several studies have shown that children are less likely to behave aggressively if they realize that a film is not real. In an experiment by Geen and Rakosky (1973), for example, a number of male students were exposed to a fictitious prizefight. In one experimental condition, the males were told that the fight was not real and that the injuries were just make-up. In the other conditions, students were not told this information. At the end of the film, the males who had been reminded of the fictional nature of the film were less aroused than the other males. This suggests that viewers who are aware that a film is fiction are less likely to take the violence seriously. They are better able to dissociate themselves from the film by reminding themselves that the images they see are not real, which may in turn affect their post-viewing aggression.

Encouraging Empathy With the Victims

A third strategy to counteract the aversive effects of media violence is to encourage children to empathize with the victims and to think about the consequences of violence from a victim's perspective. As discussed earlier, exposure to the negative consequences of violence (e.g., cries of pain, injuries) reduces the likelihood that children will learn aggressive behaviors from media characters. In a study by Nathanson and Cantor (2000), second to sixth graders were exposed to a 5-minute episode of *Woody Woodpecker*, in which Woody acts aggressively toward a man who has interrupted his nap. A third of the children were told to try and think about the feelings of the man while they viewed, another third watched the clip without any adult mediation, and a control group did not see television at all. The mediation instruction reduced the postviewing aggression scores, but only for boys and not for girls. This gender difference suggests that boys are more susceptible not only to the effects of media violence, but also to effects of strategies to counteract these effects.

Conclusion

All meta-analyses conducted so far on media effects studies have shown that media violence leads to aggression in children. Yet, it is common to read in newspapers and magazines that the effect of media violence has never been demonstrated. This chapter has shown that such claims are based on misinterpretations of empirical research, which can be explained in part by the history of academic research into the effects of media violence on aggression.

Particularly in the early stages of the research on the effects of media violence, academics had different opinions about the effects of media violence. Not only were there many academics who assumed that media violence had positive effects on children (via catharsis), but there was also a considerable group of academics who were convinced that media violence has no effect, and who made it their aim to criticize and condemn each study into the effects of media violence (e.g., see Fowles, 1999; Freedman, 1984), which is not difficult because, as discussed earlier, each type of empirical research has its weak points.

Of course, it should always be possible to discuss the value of the different types of research, but it is not right to state that the effect of media violence has never been demonstrated. This effect has been demonstrated in at least four meta-analyses and several hundred empirical studies. It is striking, though, that the researchers who have criticized the existing research most intensely have avoided the topic in their own research.

The past few years have seen several developments that have led to more consensus in the media-aggression debate, at least among academics. First, the catharsis theory was abandoned by most researchers when it became clear that the research could not yield evidence to support this hypothesis. In addition, there seems to be more agreement between researchers from different academic traditions. Cultural studies researcher David Buckingham (2000), for example, wrote in a recent book: "Of course, challenging the assumptions of effects research does not thereby mean denying the fact that the media have a degree of power to influence audiences. It is simply to suggest that the nature of that power and influence cannot be seen as a one-dimensional process of cause and effect" (p. 130).

Most media psychological effects researchers fully agree with Buckingham that the impact of media should not be seen as a unidimensional process. Most of them abandoned the model of uniform effects long ago, and are convinced that media violence is only one of the factors, and certainly not the most important one, that contribute to aggression in society. Effects researchers acknowledge that media violence can stimulate aggressive and antisocial behavior, and can desensitize children to violence in their environment. However, although media violence has no uniform effects on children, this does not mean that its influence should be denied. Just suppose that media violence negatively influences only 1% of the 75 million children and teenagers (younger than 18 years) in the United States. Such an approximation seems modest, certainly in comparison to the effect sizes that have been found in the meta-analyses. However, if only 1% of the children and teenagers in the United States were negatively affected by media violence, then the United States would have at least 750,000 young people who run the risk of a heightened level of aggression. Chance percentages of this size should be taken seriously by academics, parents, and policy makers (Bushman & Huesmann, 2001).

4

Fear Responses
to News and Entertainment

Films and news programs, especially those that portray danger, mutilations, or fearful protagonists, can provoke intense fear reactions in children. This chapter focuses on children's fear responses to audiovisual news and entertainment. The chapter consists of four sections, the first of which deals with the development of childhood fears in general. What are specific features of childhood fears and how do these develop as children mature? The second section discusses the role of audiovisual media in the development of fears, and examines which particular media contents evoke fear reactions and why. It also deals with the question of how viewers (children and adults) become afraid of particular media contents, even as they know that there is no direct danger to themselves from what they see. The third section reviews several important theories on the attraction of violent entertainment, such as the Excitation-transfer theory and the Snuggle theory. The final section concentrates on the strategies that children use to reassure themselves when they are frightened by media content, and the strategies that adults use to comfort children of different ages when they become fearful of news and entertainment media.

THE SIGNIFICANCE AND DEVELOPMENT OF CHILDHOOD FEARS

Fears, as referred to in this chapter, are seen as the subconscious and immediate responses of individuals to real or imagined dangers. Fears involve feelings of psychological discomfort, such as unease and dread, and physical responses such as perspiration and heart palpitations. These responses are generally of short duration, but sometimes they can last several hours or days, or longer. Fear responses can be examined in various ways, including interviews—by asking people how frightened they are after their viewing of a scary movie. Other methods include taking the pulse, observing facial expressions, or measuring the skin's conductivity.

People need to feel fear in order to protect themselves, to adapt to the environment, and to survive. A child who falls in the water will not simply drown. It senses the danger and does everything in its power to survive: cry for help, try to swim, anything to stay afloat. The drive for these responses is the fear of drowning (Sarafino, 1986).

Children learn about the dangers in their environment because their parents warn them. This may make them a little bit afraid. "Look both ways or you may get run over," "Don't swim too far in the sea, or you may drown," "Never swipe at a wasp, you may get stung." Only when children have learned about the potential dangers in their environment will they behave more carefully. Children who have not learned where dangers lie run the risk of, for example, of getting bitten by a dog after pulling its tail, falling out of a window while pretending to be Batman or a Pokémon, or being abducted by walking away with a stranger (Sarafino, 1986).

Fears can take various forms. It is normal for a child to be a little scared of insects, especially those that sting. But if a child panics every time an insect gets near him or her, including more innocent varieties, then something is wrong. An intense, irrational, and constant fear of specific objects or situations is called a *phobia*. In the course of time, therapists have identified hundreds of child phobias. There are, for example, phobias about the dark, animals, insects, water, heights, confined spaces, and the dentist or doctor. Phobias can be found among 2% to 3% of children, depending on the type of phobia. They are more often seen in children younger than 10 years of age, and more in girls than in boys (Anderson, Williams, McGee, & Silva, 1987; King, Gullone, & Ollendick, 1998).

Three Ways in Which Children Develop Fears

All healthy children come into the world with a number of mechanisms for protecting themselves against pain and danger. An infant, for instance, will do everything it can to remove a sheet that has fallen over his or her face, in order to make breathing easy. If the sheet stays over him or her, he or she will start to cry. This response comes from an inherent will to survive. Other responses of newborn babies are fear responses to pain, loud noises, and bright and flashing lights (Gullone, 2000).

Although many fear responses are inherent, most fears develop after birth. Newborn infants get scared of loud noises and flashing lights, but they are not likely to be frightened of monsters, the dark, or death. The majority of fears are learned. This happens in three ways. First, fear is learned through direct, personal negative experiences. For example, if a child is stung by a jellyfish when paddling in the ocean, it is very possible that later he or she will be afraid to go in the water. Fear of animals and insects often originates from a direct negative experience (King et al., 1998; Muris, Merckelbach, & Collaris, 1997; Rachman, 1991).

Fears also develop through observational learning: by watching the reactions of other people to particular situations. Imagine a young child is helping her mother clear the basement. As they move a large chest they see a mouse scurry away. The mother cries out, picks up the child, runs up the stairs and tells her daughter never to go downstairs again. The young child, at an age when she is particularly sensitive to observational learning, is frightened by her mother's reaction. She can do little else but believe that mice are terrifying creatures (Sarafino, 1986).

If children see their parents react fearfully to something, they feel that danger lies there. The underlying mechanism here is *empathy*. Empathy refers to the ability to feel the emotional reactions of others. From birth, children take on the emotions of the people around them. By means of empathy, children are able to feel fear or sadness when their parents are frightened or sad (Hoffman, 2000). It is therefore not surprising that children acquire the phobias of their parents about, for example, mice, dogs, heights, and insects.

Fears are also acquired through the transfer of negative information. A child hears a conversation in which his or her parents recount an unpleasant experience they had during a visit to a dentist. It is possible that the child may develop a fear of the dentist after hearing this story. Empathy plays a role here as well. On hearing verbal information, children have to form mental images and feel through empathy the fear that the victims have experienced (Hoffman, 2000).

Sinister jokes and warnings also fall under the category of negative information transfer. Warnings have the aim of making children a little scared to protect them from doing potentially dangerous things. Some parents can take this too far: "If you don't eat your greens, you will have to go to the doctor to have a shot"; "Not too near the water, otherwise a monster will jump out and eat you"; "Don't lie, otherwise the devil will come and take you away." It is quite possible that children develop intense fears due to these sorts of warnings.

In short, fears can be learned in three different ways: through direct negative experience, observational learning, and negative information transfer. These three causes of fear are independent but can still reinforce one another. If a child has just been bitten by a dog and later hears an unpleasant story about a dog, this can intensify his or her fear of dogs.

Which of the three causes of fear is the most common? Ollendick and King's (1991) study aimed to investigate this. They asked 1,092 American and Australian children what frightened them most. They were then asked to describe how their fear started: by direct experience, observational learning, or negative information transfer. Children named observational learning most frequently as the cause of their fear (56%). Next came negative information transfer (39%) and then personal experience (37%).

It is conceivable however, that the way in which fears are acquired differs for particular types of fear. In a study conducted by Peter Muris et al. (1997) among 129 children, the origins of fears were shown to be strongly related to the type of fear. For example, for the fear of death, negative information transfer played the most important role, but for the fear of doctors and medical operations it was direct experience. Thus it is difficult to generalize how children acquire fears. This seems to depend greatly on the type of fear that children develop.

General Trends in the Development of Childhood Fears

Although it is difficult, of course, to predict the type of fears a child may acquire, certain general trends can be identified in the development of childhood fears. A series of studies have shown that girls are generally more scared than boys. Some researchers believe that, due to certain biological gender differences, girls are born with a greater sensitivity for fear. However, the majority believes that the differences in fear found between the sexes are due to the differences in upbringing between boys and girls, or to a combination of biological gender differences and gender socialization (Gullone, 2000; Peck, 1999).

From a very early age children learn the sort of behavior that fits in with their gender. This information comes from their parents, teachers, other children, and the media. Boys are generally expected to behave in a masculine way—strong, not too emotional, logical, and adventurous. If a boy is scared, his parents tend to say that he should be a big boy, perhaps because many parents consciously or subconsciously are frightened that their son will become a bit of a sissy if they give in to his fears too much. On the other hand, when girls are emotional or show their weaknesses it is more accepted, and girls might therefore feel less inhibited than boys in admitting their fears. Research has shown that girls are comforted and reassured longer when they are afraid than boys are. They are also warned of dangers much more often, such as when climbing or swimming. It is conceivable that girls therefore develop more fears during their upbringing than boys.

The second general conclusion regarding the development of children's fears is that these fears are related to the age or the cognitive developmental level of the child. Some fears are typical for the age groups of toddlers and young children, whereas other fears develop later on in life. But why is that? One of the reasons is the way a child perceives the world changes as he or she gets older. Newborn babies live a relatively isolated life. Toddlers and young children, on the other hand, are constantly being faced with potential dangers. They happily run around with a sharp knife, in an unguarded moment put their fingers in the socket, and learn about scary monsters through fairy tales and television. Because of this, toddlers and young children not only have a greater risk of a direct experience with danger, but they are also confronted with the fears of others more often through observational learning and negative transfer of information (e.g., warnings).

Another reason for the change in the type of fears as children get older, is that their ability to think, talk, and fantasize develops strongly during the early childhood years. Up to 18-months-old, children are mainly afraid of concrete experiences, such as strangers, loud noises, and their mother disappearing from view (Gullone, 2000). Toddlers and young children, on the other hand, are able to fantasize by thinking about the things that they have done and then making predictions. This is why children of this age are particularly afraid of things in which the imagination plays a part, such as the dark, animals, and monsters (Gullone, 2000; Sarafino, 1986).

Ages 2 to 7: Crocodiles Under the Bed

From the ages of 2 to 7 the cognitive development of children makes great advances. Children increasingly use their memory and begin to make causal predictions such as "if this happens, that will happen." This is why, in addition to fears of concrete things, fears of ideas develop as well. Children become afraid of things that could happen. This brings about an increase in fears, as in the fantasy world of toddlers and young children that anything is possible. There may be a crocodile lurking underneath the bed or a ghost in the bathroom that will grab you when you run down the hallway.

The most common fears of preschoolers involve large animals (that can eat you) and insects (that can crawl over you). Eighty percent of 5- and 6-year-olds say that they are afraid of some sort of animal. Following in second place are monsters. Almost three fourths of preschoolers say that they are scared of monsters and the like, including witches, giants, and trolls. Finally, children in this age group are often afraid of the dark, doctors and dentists, deep water, great heights, and of everything that looks strange or makes sudden movements (Bauer, 1976; Cantor, 2002; Maurer, 1965; Muris, Merckelbach, Gadet, & Moulaert, 2000).

Children up to approximately 4 years of age believe that inanimate objects are alive. The sun lives because it gives off light, the vacuum cleaner because it eats dust, and the oven is alive because it makes food. Everything that does something or serves a useful purpose is alive. These animistic convictions just add to the list of children's fears. Children of 2 and 3 years of age may be afraid to get eaten up by the vacuum cleaner because they see the vacuum as a monster that moves and roars around the room. Sometimes 2- and 3-year-olds are afraid of disappearing down the toilet or getting sucked down the drain of the bathtub. The reason for this is, at this age, children do not realize that big, solid objects do not fit into smaller ones (Fraiberg, 1959).

Ages 7 to 10: Earthquakes and Burglars

When children are 7 they are reasonably able to make distinctions between fantasy and reality when processing information. This ability is shown in their fears. The fear of monsters quickly reduces when children turn 7. Compared with 5- and 6-year-olds the fear of monsters in 7- and 8-year-olds will have already been reduced by one third to one half (Bauer, 1976; Maurer, 1965; Muris et al., 2000).

The typical infant and toddler fears are replaced by other fears. A fear often seen in children of 7 to 10 years of age is the fear of illnesses or physical harm and the fear of losing people whom they love. They also become afraid of realistic threats, such as accidents, abductions, burglars, bombardments, and natural disasters.

From 10 Onward: Exams, Wars, and Global Warming

The emotional life of children from 10 years and older is still characterized by fear of physical harm, but a concern for social relationships also begins to develop. Teenagers and 10- to 12-year-olds become afraid of rejection by parents, teachers, and their peers. They also start to compare themselves with their peers, which may make them feel inferior in certain respects. When teenagers feel that they are not doing as well in comparison to others, they may become shy and afraid of too much public attention. Finally, children at this age develop fears of abstract things, such as politics and the economy, the global situation, and wars and nuclear weapons (Cantor, Wilson, & Hoffner, 1986; Gullone, 2000).

Raising Children Without Fears Is an Illusion

It is impossible to raise children without fear. This is clearly illustrated in the anecdote about Frankie in the famous book *The Magical Years* by Selma Fraiberg (1959). Frankie was a toddler who had to be an example of a modern, scientifically raised child. In the pedagogic program that his parents had written for him, all possible sources of fears had been systematically eradicated. Nursery rhymes and fairy tales had all been modified. Giants did not eat people, but cookies. And witches, monsters, and the like had only harmless habits.

Sometimes they made a little slip, but then they quickly bettered themselves. Nobody died in the fairy tales or in Frankie's real life. When his bird died, his parents secretly put a new one in the cage so that Frankie never noticed the loss.

Yet Frankie became scared. When he was 2 he was afraid to be sucked down the drain of the bathtub, just like many other children. When Frankie reached the age when many other children wake up from nightmares he, too, began to wake up from these frightening dreams, and despite his parents' very carefully planned pedagogic program, Frankie was being pursued in his dreams by a giant who wanted to eat him.

That was not all. Despite the light treatment the witches and monsters received in Frankie's upbringing, the villains in his own stories met a much more unpleasant end. In his dreams Frankie got rid of the witches and giants by chopping off their heads.

This story about Frankie illustrates that it is impossible to raise children without fear. Even if adults do everything in their power to eradicate frightening witches and ghosts from children's stories, a child will still create his or her own scary fantasies. And there is a good reason for it: fears play an important part in the development of a child. In their childhood, children have to overcome numerous fears, but it is because of this that they develop confidence. If children can overcome fears on their own, they will begin to feel independent. They will feel that they have control over the events in their lives. On the other hand, if a child at an early age is faced with too great a fear, that goes beyond his or her ability to deal with, he or she will feel helpless, powerless, and inferior, and may develop a negative self-image (Fraiberg, 1959).

Children are equipped with a number of tools to overcome their fears. According to Fraiberg (1959), when children are 2 years old, they already have a psychological system that gives them the ability to anticipate, evaluate, and conquer fears. Whether they use these tools successfully depends on the way that their parents teach them to use them.

Most experts agree that a little fear is necessary for a healthy mental development. But they also agree that being confronted with shocking events goes far beyond a child's processing ability and has a negative effect on a healthy mental development. What are the consequences for contact with television, the medium that confronts young children with dozens of realistically filmed murders and acts of violence on a daily basis? Are children capable of dealing with horror movies and realistic news footage at an early age? This question is answered in the next section of this chapter.

THE ROLE OF MASS MEDIA IN THE DEVELOPMENT OF FEARS

Films and news programs can evoke intense fears in children and adults. The fact that such fears can in some cases deeply affect people is illustrated by anecdotes about the impact of movies such as *Jaws* and *Psycho*. In the summer that *Jaws* came out, various American newspapers reported that the beaches were remarkably empty. They suspected that the crowds stayed away out of fear of being attacked by an enormous great white shark. The infamous scene from the movie *Psycho*, in which a woman is killed while she is in the shower, also left its mark. Never had so many transparent shower curtains been sold as when *Psycho* was shown in the movie theaters. In this second section, I further examine the role that mass media plays in the development of fears. I look at children's fear responses to entertainment designed for adults, to entertainment aimed at children, and to news.

Fear Responses to Entertainment Designed for Adults

The interest in fear responses of children to violent entertainment has grown in recent years. This interest has developed not only because entertainment designed for adults has become more realistic and gruesome, but also because children and adolescents are increasingly regarded as a target group for this kind of entertainment. This trend began in the 1950s, when comic books, extremely popular at that time, started to add horror pictures in a way that appealed to male adolescents. This change turned out to be very lucrative. Even the black and white images on newly-available television could not compete with the macabre pictures and bright colors of the gory horror comic strips (Tamborini & Weaver, 1996).

The movie industry soon discovered a target group that had time and money to spend: the youngsters who read those horror comic strips. *The Curse of Frankenstein* in 1957 led to a series of low-budget films with similar themes, in which the camera, unlike films of the past, did not shy away from showing atrocities and horror. After several years, the limited success of these films got the attention of renowned filmmakers such as Alfred Hitchcock. This resulted in *Psycho* in 1960. *Psycho* is considered by historically oriented media researchers as the turning point in the production of horror movies. Due to its overwhelming success, the film led to a flood of imitations, and so the prestige of Hitchcock legitimized the arrival of a new kind of horror movie: movies with macabre murders and realistically filmed mutilations (Sapolsky & Molitor, 1996; Tamborini & Weaver, 1996).

What is the effect of this new generation of violent entertainment on children? This is difficult to assess, as the scientific research into the fear responses of children presents a number of serious problems that make it difficult to draw any conclusions on the negative effects. The main problem is that for ethical reasons, it is impossible, to use experiments to determine the extent to which children experience fear from extreme types of violent entertainment. You can hardly show children a gory, violent movie to assess their fear in the name of science. This means that the scientific conclusions about fear responses of children to media are mainly based on anecdotes, in-depth interviews, case studies, questionnaire studies, and experiments that use relatively mild forms of violence to show differences between conditions (Cantor, 2002).

Young children often watch programs that adults consider intensely terrifying. A study by Sparks (1986) revealed, for example, that one half of the 4- to 10-year-olds that he studied have seen the movies *Poltergeist* and *Jaws*. In a survey conducted by Hoekstra, Harris, and Helmick (1999), 61% of a group of American students said that they had experienced intense and lengthy fear responses in their youth. Of these students, 29% stated that they have a specific fear left from an audiovisual production, such as fear of sharks or spiders, and 20% reported suffering from a variety of sleeping disorders, such as a fear of sleeping alone, nightmares, insomnia, or the need to leave a light on at night.

To examine how often Dutch children are afraid when watching entertainment designed for adults, I studied 314 7- to 12-year-olds with coresearchers Joanne Cantor and Allerd Peeters (Valkenburg, Cantor, & Peeters, 2000). We asked them whether they had been scared by watching a movie or a television program in the last year so much that it bothered them afterward. Thirty-one percent of the children said that had happened. Almost all children who had a long-term fear named a film for adults as the source of their fear.

As mentioned earlier, it is not unusual that children are a little frightened now and again by something they see in the media. However, it is a different story when children are affected for a long time by something they have seen. This circumstance could indicate that the content has been too much for these children to handle and that a form of traumatization has occurred. How long did the children in our study stay frightened as a result of something they had seen on television? For most children (79%) who had been frightened in the previous year, the fear was gone within several hours or days. But for 21% the fear stayed for weeks or even months afterward. The most common responses of these children were: talking a lot and asking questions about the program, afraid of going to bed, waking up during the night, and bad dreams and nightmares.

Our study examined the question of how often the children had been afraid of something they had seen on television in the last year. It is possible that a child was not scared that particular year but became scared a year later. How often have people who grew up with television been intensely afraid of a television program at least once in their childhood? To find out, I asked a group of communication science students to write down whether they had experienced such a fear, and if so, which movie or program frightened them. I also asked them how old they were at the time and what their response was. Some of the students' descriptions are included in this chapter using fictitious names.

Of the 75 students who took part in the study, more than 70% could remember a specific movie or program on television that frightened them intensely. The age at which this fear surfaced varied greatly, as well as the kind of programs that caused the fear. As was the case in earlier studies by Joanne Cantor and her colleagues (e.g., Cantor, 2002), the type of movie was closely related to the age. The scariest program for young children was the television series *The Incredible Hulk*. Reality programs and horror movies such as *Jaws*, *It*, and *Child's Play* caused fear in older children and adolescents.

> That little doll Chucky. It was a scary, ugly doll in any case. But it got even scarier when it showed its teeth and rolled its eyes, and started to bite ... It said: "Hi, I'm Chucky, I'm your friend till the end of time." I'll never forget those words. Afterwards I got scared of my own dolls. For months I slept badly, had scary dreams. And still, when I see an ugly doll, I think about Chucky. (Joanne, 22, about the movie *Child's Play*)

With most students, the fear caused by the movie or the program was gone after a few days or weeks. But with some students there were more serious effects: No less than 12% were troubled by fears for years due to a specific movie. And more than half of these students regretted, in retrospect, having seen the program concerned. One student said that after 20 years she still sometimes wakes up drenched in sweat because of a movie she had seen as a 5-year-old:

> I don't remember the title of the movie, but there was a plague of ants in a town. Everything, people and animals, even elephants were being attacked and eaten. First the arms. Then the head and finally the body. Running was futile ... I was five when I saw the movie. Afterwards I often dreamt that I was being crushed by something that grew ever larger, just like the group of ants that got bigger and bigger. My aversion to insects may well be because of this film. Even a single ant on the kitchen worktop will start my heart pounding. (Sandy, 25)

In scientific and political circles, the discussion about violent entertainment looks mainly at the consequences of violence on aggressive behavior rather than on fear. This is hardly surprising, because aggression among youngsters is an important social problem. In the past 15 years alone, juvenile crime has increased dramatically, and aggressive youngsters are more of a nuisance to society than frightened ones. People generally tend to keep their fears, as well as their fantasies, to themselves. Young children show that they are scared, but teenagers, and boys in particular, prefer to keep this feeling to themselves. Several studies have shown that the effects of television on fear are sometimes underestimated. After my lectures about fear and the media, my students sometimes tell me that they were troubled by fears when they were teenagers, but they never talked about it at the time:

I never told anyone how scared I was. During the day I'd laugh at it. I used to enjoy scaring the life out of my younger sister by enacting scenes from the film. But at night it would haunt me. I was afraid to switch off the light. And when it was off, I was afraid to switch it back on, I was afraid I would feel the hand of the devil instead of the light switch .... For years I was terrified in bed. At times when it was really bad, I would put garlic under my pillow. I was often exhausted in the morning. I would then play truant for the first hour. I had to repeat a year. I'm sure that *The Exorcist* played a major role in this .... (Sylvia, 22)

Fear Responses to Children's Entertainment

Entertainment made especially for children, as well as that made for adults, contains a great deal of violence. For much of the children's entertainment (e.g., cartoons) it is assumed that children of all ages can watch them without any negative effect. In reality this is not always true. Some of these so-called "family movies" are packed with physical and psychological violence. I once interviewed a father who told me that one Saturday afternoon he had taken his 4-year-old son to see *Lion King*. In this movie the lion cub, Simba, witnesses how his father is tragically crushed by stampeding bison. After 5 minutes his son was sitting on the floor between the seats, shivering with fear. Ten minutes later they were outside. The child was upset for the rest of the day.

Contrary to what is often assumed, many children's and family movies are not suitable for young children. Family movies such as *Lion King* are often only suitable for children who are able to comfort themselves by reasoning that what they see is "only make believe." Children younger than the age of 7 can not do this, and even if an adult watches with them, this kind of family movie can still frighten them intensely and for a long period of time (see also Cantor, 1998a).

Fear Responses to News

Until now, there has been very little scientific research into fear responses to the news. The first study on this subject, conducted by Cantor and Nathanson, was published in 1996. This survey found that 37% of American children between the ages of 5 and 12 sometimes become and remain scared from watching the news. This percentage is slightly higher in Dutch children. In a survey conducted with Juliette Walma van der Molen and Allerd Peeters, we asked 500 7- to 12-year-olds whether they had ever felt so scared after watching the news that the feeling remained for some time. Forty-eight percent of them said that they sometimes remained scared after watching the news, a percentage very similar to that found by Cantor and Nathanson for the same age group. Table 4.1 shows the subjects in the news that children found particularly frightening. The percentages in the table are based on children's spontaneous answers.

As can be seen in the table, interpersonal violence was the biggest cause of children's fear. In second place were fires, accidents, and disasters. Wars and burglaries were also often mentioned. And finally, a number of children got upset when other children or animals were harmed. There were several differences between younger and older children. Seven- to eight-year-olds tended to name fires, accidents and disasters, whereas the 9- to 12-year-olds were more often afraid of wars. This is probably because the ability to think abstractly is more developed in older children than in younger ones. With fear of wars, older children will think more about the consequences for the people in the country at war than younger children (Hoffman, 2000; Walma van der Molen et al., 2002).

How do Children Become Frightened by Media Content?

Earlier in this chapter, I described that fears can develop in three ways: through direct experience, observational learning, and negative information transfer. In the next sections, I examine the extent to which each of these three ways can be used to explain the fear responses of children to what they see in the media. It becomes clear that they play a major role.

Direct Experience Via Stimulus Generalization

Imagine you are going for a walk in a beautiful tropical wood somewhere in Indonesia. The sun shines through the trees and a group of monkeys are happily

TABLE 4.1

Topics in the News That Frighten Younger and Older Children

	7- to 8-year-olds %*	9- to 12-year-olds %*
Interpersonal violence	40	51
Fires, accidents and disasters	34	21
War	14	23
Burglary and theft	9	6
Children who get hurt	3	11
Animals who get hurt	6	4

Note. Adapted from Walma van der Molen et al., 2002.

*The percentages do not add up because children could mention more than one topic.

playing above you on the branches. Suddenly, a few feet away, you see an enormous snake slithering toward you, its head raised. You are scared stiff: a normal human fear response, caused by a direct negative experience with danger.

But now imagine you are watching a movie on television one evening and you see a similar situation. Will you be afraid? You are, after all, safe in your living room where there are no snakes. This may seem peculiar in theory, and yet these kinds of scenes often evoke an intense fear. How is that possible? How can it be that people become frightened of things they see in the media when they know that there is no direct danger for themselves in what they see?

Danger in the media seems primarily to evoke direct fear, in the same way as danger frightens someone in reality. According to Joanne Cantor (1991) certain situations have been frightening people from the beginning of time. These are natural disasters, earthquakes, and epidemics; attacks by dangerous animals or people; physical mutilation; and people or animals that look unnatural, such as people who have been mutilated, people with a physical deformity, and monsters. According to Cantor the fear responses evoked by these kinds of danger are involuntary and deeply embedded in every person.

Cantor (1991) assumes that the stimuli that have been evoking fear since our early human history do the same when we are faced with them in the media. She believes this occurs through stimulus generalization, a concept she derives from classic conditioning theory. This theory assumes that when a stimulus evokes an emotional reaction, other closely related stimuli evoke similar but less intensive emotional reactions. The stimulus generalization principle therefore predicts that a media stimulus very similar to the actual stimulus brings about a similar, but less intense reaction than the actual stimulus. In short, the process of stimulus generalization has to be regarded as the media variant of acquired fears through direct experience.

Observational Learning of Fears From Media Characters

Fear responses to what is seen in the media can also arise through observational learning: by observing the emotional reactions to dangers of main characters or victims in media productions. In audio-visual media productions it is very common to show fear through the fear experienced by the main characters or victims. The danger itself is often not even shown; the emotional reactions of television characters are enough to bring about an intense fear response in the viewer. According to Bandura (1994) these kinds of emotional reactions of media characters can cause short-term as well as permanent fear in viewers.

An experiment conducted by Venn and Short (1973) confirms that observational learning of fear through television characters occurs in young children. These researchers showed a number of 3- and 4-year-olds a short film in which a mother shows a plastic Mickey Mouse doll to her 5-year-old son. Each time the boy in the film sees the doll, he screams with fear. When his mother shows him a plastic Donald Duck doll, he is not frightened at all. He is perfectly relaxed and even smiles a little at the doll. After the children watched the film, the researchers played a game in which both the Mickey Mouse and the Donald Duck doll were used. The film had a clear effect on the children: They did not mind playing with Donald Duck but stayed well away from Mickey Mouse.

Empathy plays a major role in the observational learning of fear from media characters. The emotional response that the viewer gets with empathy is related to the emotion of the observed character. Viewers feel sad when a main character in a movie is sad and experience fear when he or she is scared. A main character or victim does not even have to show fear to frighten viewers. Viewers can also become scared when the main characters are unaware of the impending danger. This instrument of the *naive main character* is fairly common in fiction. Take for example a movie scenario in which a female character walks in the woods. The camera shows the viewer a dangerous monster lurking in the shadows, waiting for the moment to attack the unsuspecting woman. In these cases viewers are often on the edge of their seats with fear. This sort of scene lacks the emotion of the movie character, and yet empathy plays a part. In literature this phenomenon whereby empathy is felt without actually seeing the emotions of the character is called *anticipatory empathy* (Stotland, 1969). It refers to the emotions that a viewer feels when he or she realizes that another person's emotional reactions are imminent.

Negative Information Transfer

A third way in which children and adults can acquire fears through the media is through negative information transfer. No one will deny that audio-visual media are packed with negative information. A large part of the news deals with crime, wars, and other dangers. Television news is given to us through images but also for a large part through the newsreader, reports of news correspondents or the eyewitness accounts of victims. This verbal information from the newsreader or the reports and eyewitness accounts are examples of negative information transfer.

Negative information transfer does not occur only through the news. Theoretically, this can happen through fiction as well. It has been found on various occasions that people's fear and their estimation of the probability of becoming a victim of crime is related to the frequency of their viewing television dramas (Gerbner, Gross, Morgan, & Signorielli, 1994). Although it is not known how often people pick up negative information from television dramas, it is possible that negative information transfer during both news and fiction plays a role in the development of fear.

Fears Caused by Fiction: The Law of Apparent Reality

What is seen in the media can evoke fear. This applies not only to news programs but also to fiction. The fact that people become frightened because of the news through the aforementioned three processes is understandable. News, after all, concerns reality, and one takes that seriously. But why do these processes take place with fictitious media content, with things that could never happen in reality? Why are both children and adults often as receptive to frightening scenes in fictitious stories as in the news? In order to understand this phenomenon principles from the general emotion literature may be of use.

Emotion researchers assume that the intensity of an emotional reaction depends on the reality status of the stimulus that evokes the emotional reaction. Paul Harris (2000) gave a clear example: When we hear a fire alarm, we feel fear. If the alarm turns out to be a false alarm, the fear disappears. This means that the intensity of the emotions experienced is related to the perceived realism of the threat. Nico Frijda (1988) tried to incorporate this emotion characteristic in a psychological law: the law of apparent reality. This law states that emotions are triggered by events that the individual regards as realistic and that the intensity of this emotion corresponds to the degree to which the events are perceived as realistic.

The law of apparent reality is plausible but it does rule out that one can experience emotions while watching fiction. Take, for example, a science fiction movie such as *Alien*, in which a man in excruciating pain has a baby monster burst out of his stomach. Such a scene is far removed from reality but still has the capacity to evoke strong fear responses. Why do viewers not respond to such a fiction as they would when hearing a false fire alarm? This problem in Frijda's law of apparent reality was raised by Walters (1989) and was then acknowledged a year later by Frijda. In a follow-up article Frijda (1989) gave an explanation for why people experience emotions with fictitious stories. He stated that viewers regard movies as true events in a fantasy world. Viewers do not perceive the occurrence as unreal; they ignore any proof in the movie that points to it being unreal. They voluntarily suspend, as it were, their disbelief. According to Frijda this can only occur when a movie is realistic enough to allow for this suspension.

Harris (2000) gave another explanation for the recurrence of aesthetic emotions—emotions in response to fictitious media. Harris agreed with Frijda that perceived reality is a precondition for feeling emotions, also aesthetic emotions. However, he felt that Frijda's law of apparent reality is not comprehensive enough. Harris believed that fiction can be consumed by viewers in two ways. First, is the default mode, whereby viewers do not employ their knowledge of the reality status of the movie in order to suppress their emotions. In this default mode viewers are emotionally touched by movies, not because they constantly think that the movie is real, but because they do not include their knowledge of the reality status of the movie in their evaluation.

In the second way that viewers consume fiction, they do use this knowledge of the reality status of the movie. Sometimes they do this resolutely; for example, when they see a shocking scene such as a mutilation. The viewers then try not to be open to the image and say to themselves that the mutilation is "only pretend." Using the knowledge about the reality status of fiction can also occur subconsciously; for example, when the characters act unconvincingly. In both cases the reality of the production is doubted, and the corresponding emotional responses are immediately decreased.

However, the question has to be answered of why we process fictitious dangers usually in default mode; that is to say, with corresponding emotions. Harris (2000) offered an explanation of this process using an evolutionary theory. At some point in our evolution man acquired the capacity to use language. Initially language was probably used for communication about the here and now: for example, to show someone the location of edible plants or herbs in the surrounding area, or to co-ordinate a hunt. At some point, language was used for other purposes. People transferred information that was received in other places at another time: They started to rely on eyewitness accounts. Of course these eyewitness accounts sometimes contained emotionally charged events, such as someone describing how her son had died in excruciating pain after eating a particular fruit. To understand these kinds of accounts, the listeners had to form a mental image of the fruit and the serious implications if it should be eaten. With that mental image they felt emotions.

What if this kind of information had left our ancestors cold? And they could only respond emotionally if they had experienced the situation themselves? Not only would we have very limited social relationships, but we would not be able to respond quickly to other people's warnings, nor be able to anticipate the dangers that the eyewitnesses pointed out to us. The aim of the warnings of eyewitnesses, after all, was to frighten us, to prevent mistakes being repeated. These communicative skills, as well as the ability to re-enact in one's mind these eyewitness accounts, have had enormous consequences for the development of man. According to Harris (2000), our emotional involvement with fiction is an inheritance of beings who use language and who can form mental re-enactments from eyewitness accounts. He believes that our negative emotional responses to drama and fiction is a small evolutionary price that we have to pay for our interest and emotional openness to accounts of eyewitnesses.

Factors That Increase Fear of Media Content

There are a number of factors that can increase the fear of what is seen in the media. These factors are to do with characteristics of the media production itself as well as those of the viewer. In the following I describe six factors that apply to both children and adults.

Resemblance of Media Content to Reality. Both the stimulus generalization theory and the law of apparent reality suggest that the closer a danger in the media is to reality, the greater the fear experienced by the viewer. Research has shown that this is indeed the case. For example, adults become more scared of violence used by people of flesh and blood than of violence by cartoon or animation characters (Gunter & Furnham, 1984). This also applies to children. In a study conducted by Osborn and Endsley (1971) children said that they found a program with human violence more frightening than one in which the same violence was perpetrated by puppets.

Whether a stimulus is close to reality or not depends not only on the characteristics of the movie but also on the way the viewers perceive it. The radio play *The War of the Worlds* by H. G. Wells, already referred to in the first chapter, is a clear example of this. This play, broadcast one October evening in 1938 in the United States, is a realistic account of an invasion of North America by extraterrestrials. Even before the radio broadcast had finished it became clear how intensely scared the listeners had been. Many people who listened to the radio that evening thought that what they had heard was really happening. Large numbers called neighbors and family to warn them of the invasion. And many fled into the streets in sheer panic.

Cantril (1940) studied these responses of the listeners to find out what it was in the broadcast that had frightened them so much. The program had been very realistic, mainly due to the convincing way the authorities were portrayed in the radio play. Many listeners had missed the announcement at the start of the program that informed them that this was a radio play. Others thought that the play had been interrupted by a news program about the invasion. In short, this classic and, for communication scientists and media psychologists, very interesting incident makes it clear how strong the relation is between people's perception of reality and their emotional responses to the media.

Connection of Media Content With Existing Fears. Things shown in the media that connect with an individual's existing fears will have a higher emotional impact. For example, a child who is already afraid of spiders will become even more scared when watching a movie such as *Arachnophobia*, in which a village is terrorized by an army of poisonous tarantulas. This resonance process has been confirmed by research. Experiments have shown that people who are afraid of dying are relatively more scared when they watch a movie about a fatal disease than people who fear death to a lesser degree or not at all (Weiss, Katkin, & Rubin, 1968). It has also been shown that women who have just had babies have a higher pulse when watching a movie about a birth than women who have not just given birth (Sapolsky & Zillmann, 1978).

The Geographical Proximity of the Place of the Media Danger.   Another factor that can increase fear is the relative closeness of the place or context of the media danger. Incidents that occur geographically close to the viewer have in general a higher impact than incidents that happen far away. This applies to both news and entertainment. In an experiment conducted by Heath (1984) groups of students were allocated to two experimental conditions in which a movie showed a crime being committed. Half the participants were told that the crime had been committed in the area, and the other half, that it had been committed in a city far away. The students who thought that the crime had been committed in the area were more afraid than the other students. An experiment conducted by Smith and Wilson (2000) showed that 10- and 11-year-old children were more afraid of news about a crime that had been committed in their city than of news about a crime far away.

Motivation to be Open to Fear.   The motives of the viewers to watch media dangers play a role as well. As explained earlier in this chapter, viewers can apply various cognitive viewing strategies. They can watch fiction purely for entertainment or to get a kick out of it. If it is the latter, they can increase the emotional impact of the movie on themselves by choosing to believe what takes place in the movie. Zillmann (1982) called this process the *willing suspension of disbelief.* Apparently people sometimes enjoy getting emotionally carried away while watching fiction. Contrary cognitive viewing processes also take place. Adult viewers who want to limit the emotional impact can concentrate on the thought that the events are taking place within the confines of the media production, so that they do not take them seriously. This ability of older children and adults is called adult discount (Zillmann, 1982).

Characteristics of the Movie.   Film producers use a number of stylistic tools to increase the effect of fear in fiction. Himmelweit, Oppenheim, and Vince (1958) found that children felt certain sound effects, particularly music, were frightening elements in movies. Thayer and Levinson (1983) showed that adding different kinds of music to a movie can increase or decrease the fear responses. They found that adding so-called horror music to a documentary about industrial accidents led to more fear than when the usual standard documentary music was used. Also certain announcements prior to the program informing the viewer of the shocking scenes in the movie, thereby preparing the viewer for a bloody murder, appeared to lead to more fear responses than with films in which the bloody massacre came as a surprise (Nomikos, Opton, Avetrill, & Lazarus, 1968).

Cognitive Developmental Level of the Viewer.   The cognitive developmental level of a viewer is an important determining factor for the intensity of the fear of media dangers. Children up to approximately 6-years-old are not yet quite capable of deploying the adult discount as previously described. In other words, they can neither adequately apply their knowledge as to what is and is not fantasy while watching fiction, nor can they effectively comfort themselves by thinking that what they see is only "make believe." Telling children who are 6-years-old that what they see is not real, works well. Only later are children able to employ this knowledge without help (Harris, 2000). This special characteristic of young children has great consequences for their processing of fictitious media. This is discussed further in the next section.

Age Differences in Fears of Media Content

Although it is difficult to predict which specific programs or fragments of programs evoke fear in an individual child, some general rules can be identified in the development of fears in children. Age or cognitive level is not only an important predictor of the fears that children develop in daily life, but also of the events in the media that frighten children. On the basis of her research into the influence of media on fears in children, Cantor (2002) came to three general conclusions.

Fantastic Versus Realistic Media Content. The first conclusion is that children up until the age of 7 are mainly scared of fantastic dangers in the media, of events that can not happen in reality. They can also get upset by things that suddenly disappear or acquire another form, something that often happens in cartoons. As of 7 years of age the fear of fantastic dangers reduces. Although children from that moment on can still be scared from watching fictitious media, the fictional situations have to be able to take place in real life to evoke fear (e.g., *X-files*; *Miami Vice*).

> When I was 5, I was terrified of *The Incredible Hulk*. That man changing into the Hulk has left a long-lasting impression on me. When in bed at night, I would insist on leaving the door open. I was petrified that the Hulk would come into my room with those white eyes of his. This fear lasted several months. When I see *The Incredible Hulk* on television now, it just cracks me up. (Pauline, 21)

Perceptual Versus Conceptual Processing of Media. Cantor's (2002) second conclusion is that young children tend to become more easily frightened of movies with clearly visible dangers, such as *The Wizard of Oz*, whereas older children are more scared of movies that have implied or suggested dangers, such as *Poltergeist*. In the movie *Poltergeist* the inhabitants of a haunted house are being terrorized by ghosts. Many dangers in this movie are often implied by suggested dangers: scary music and shifting furniture suggest to the viewer that the poltergeist is lurking somewhere. Young children often may not understand these kinds of dangers. They see a table move around, but do not associate this with the poltergeist. Children need to have a certain knowledge of these kinds of implied dangers, a knowledge that they often do not yet have (Cantor, 2002).

Concrete Versus Abstract Dangers. Cantor's (2002) third and final conclusion is that television movies or programs with abstract dangers are particularly scary for older children. Movies with abstract dangers are about political invasions, sinister conspiracies, disasters with poisonous gas, and so forth. A good example of this is the movie *The Day After* about a nuclear attack on an American community. When this movie was shown on television in the United States, many parents worried about the reactions of their children. Research conducted by Cantor, Wilson, and Hoffner (1986) shows, however, that children up to 12 were less upset than were teenagers. In fact, the parents were shocked the most. The reason for this is that the emotional effects of this movie are particularly evoked by the speculation regarding the possible destruction of the earth. This is an abstract concept that young children do not grasp. Sensing danger depends on knowledge and experience. An attack by an animal evokes fear in everybody, as it calls on instinctive reactions to fast approaching objects, sudden or strange movements, and loud noises. But for other threats, such as nuclear weapons, a certain knowledge is required that is lacking in young children (Cantor, 2002; Cantor, et al., 1986).

"BUT IT IS ALSO A BIT OF FUN" TO WATCH MEDIA VIOLENCE

I remember a story an old neighbor once told me. He had witnessed a traffic accident in which a heavily loaded truck had run over a cyclist. It was horrible. Within minutes masses of people had come to the scene of the accident. My neighbor described his experience as follows: "On the one hand it had intensely scared and horrified me. I had to vomit and wanted to run away. But at the same time I had some kind of morbid curiosity to see what would happen next." There are not many things as paradoxical as watching violence—whether in reality or through the media. On the one hand viewers can become intensely frightened from watching certain elements in media productions. And yet they want to watch it over and over again. That also applies to children. In one of my studies no less than 53% of the children who in the last year had been frightened by something on television, indicated they also found it "a bit of fun" to watch scary things. Eight percent even liked it very much to watch scary programs on television.

The need to see violence and terrifying things is something that is deeply rooted in the human psyche. Take, for example, the gladiator fights in the amphitheaters of Rome 2,000 years ago. Gladiators, usually prisoners of war or slaves, fought to the death against wild animals or each other. They were often torn apart by lions or crocodiles while tens of thousands of spectators cheered excitedly. Why do adults and children enjoy watching violent and terrifying movies, even if afterward they remain frightened, have problems sleeping, and get nightmares? This is something scientists are still studying and to which there is no single answer. There are several theories, five of which I discuss.

Excitation-Transfer Theory

The first explanation for the enjoyment people derive from watching violence is offered by the excitation-transfer theory of Zillmann (1978). This theory assumes that every emotion (e.g., fear, anger, joy) brings about in people similar kinds of arousal. This arousal varies in intensity, but is in terms of quality no different for the various emotions. Another principle of the excitation-transfer theory is that when two events that both bring about a heightened state of arousal occur after one another, the arousal created by the first event can intensify the arousal resulting from the next event.

So what does this have to do with watching violence? When a child watches something terrifying, such as a murder scene, his or her arousal will rise as a result of a fear response. When the terrifying scene is then finished—for example, because the victim manages to escape—the child experiences a new emotion: relief. However, because the child is still in the heightened state of arousal, and because this excitement is followed by a new emotion, the feeling of relief is especially intense. In other words, children who had first been a little afraid of something seen in the movie, feel more relieved and satisfied when the danger has gone. And it is this relief intensified by arousal that makes watching violence so appealing.

Sensation Seeking Theory

According to sensation seeking theory, children and adults enjoy watching violent and terrifying programs because it satisfies their need for sensation. The psychological concept of sensation seeking is defined by Zuckerman (1996) as people's tendency to search for varied, new, complex, and intense sensations and experiences and their willingness to take physical, social, legal, and financial risks to experience these sensations. From long ago people have had a need for sensation, some more than others. According to Zuckerman (1979) the need for sensation increases during childhood. It peaks during the teenage years and then gradually decreases with age. Generally speaking boys have a greater need for sensation than girls.

Children and teenagers are therefore relatively avid sensation seekers. What do they do with this need for excitement and sensation? This differs by child. Young children wrestle around or play superheroes. Teenagers with a strong need for sensation may try, for example, bungee jumping. But children can also satisfy their need for sensation by watching action and horror movies. The preference of children and young people for terrifying media content is indeed connected to their need for sensation. A study by Johnston (1995) revealed that high school students with a strong need for sensation enjoyed horror movies more than their peers with a low need for sensation did.

Forbidden-Fruit Theory

A third reason why children are attracted to violent media content is that they enjoy participating in exciting and aggressive behavior in a vicarious way; behavior for which they are either too young to carry out successfully, or simply too young to be allowed. Many adventure and action movies show scenes in which social standards are transgressed. It may well be that children enjoy participating vicariously in the behavior of superheroes ignoring social norms (Cantor, 1998b; Sparks & Sparks, 2000).

Snuggle Theory

This theory suggests that adolescents find violent entertainment appealing because it offers them the opportunity to discover and reinforce their gender roles. Boys can show that they are masculine and girls can demonstrate that they admire boys for it. This theory elaborates on observations of the Roman philosopher Ovid (43 BC–18 AD) during the violent gladiator fights in the Colosseum of the ancient Rome, where male and female spectators would have had the opportunity to meet one another. In his *Ars Amatoria*, the first western manual for the art of seduction, Ovid explained the social function of the gladiator fights. The more gruesome the fights were the more physical comfort women sought from the men. Women shuddered with fear during the fights and held on tightly to the men in complete subordination. According to Ovid it was this subordinate position of women that was the cause of romantic attraction and sexual favors (Zillmann & Gibson, 1996).

According to Zillmann, Weaver, Mundorf, and Aust (1986) violent and terrifying entertainment is still considered appealing due to its gender role-socialization function. This kind of entertainment offers men the opportunity to prove their courage and masculinity, whereas it gives women the opportunity to show their sensitivity and need for protection. In order to test their snuggle theory, Zillmann et al. showed a group of first-year students extracts of the movie *Friday the 13th, Part III.* Each subject watched together with a student of the opposite sex. These persons paired off with the students pretended to be objective viewers, but were in actual fact allies of the researchers. While watching, these allies displayed different behavior with different students. With one group of students they were indifferent, with a second group "in control," and with a third group emotional. After the movie the subjects had to indicate what they thought of the movie. As the researchers had expected, male students liked the movie best when they had watched it together with an "emotional" woman. The female students, on the other hand, enjoyed the movie best when they had watched it with a man who was in control.

The "Me Too" Effect

Some children watch scary movies so that they can later talk about the details in the movie. If a movie or program is "hip" at school, you have to see it as well. An illustrative example here is the series *Faces of Death*, which caused some commotion in the mid-1990s in the Netherlands. In *Faces of Death* living dogs were cut open, bank directors shot in the head, and bungee-jumpers fell to the ground, all of which was real-life footage. Members of Parliament dared not watch the movie on their own, finding it too gruesome. And yet one in three students had seen one or more episodes of the series. If classmates talk so much about it, you *must*, of course, see it as well (Cantor, 1998b).

COPING STRATEGIES TO REDUCE MEDIA-INDUCED FRIGHT

As mentioned earlier, during childhood children progressively learn to cope with fears, including media-induced fears. Children generally use two types of reassurance strategies: cognitive and noncognitive. With cognitive strategies, children try to reason their fear away, such as by telling themselves that what they see is only make believe, that blood on television is only paint or ketchup, or that they are too old to be afraid. Noncognitive strategies are physical intervention strategies, like closing one's eyes, hiding behind the couch or switching off the television, as well as social intervention strategies, such as going to sit on a parent's lap or getting a doll or cuddly toy. As of 9 years of age children mainly use cognitive strategies to comfort themselves, whereas younger children primarily find reassurance in noncognitive ways (Cantor, 2002; Valkenburg & Cantor, 2000).

Ways to Comfort Children in the Case of Violent News and Entertainment

Children have a number of tools to help them overcome their fears. Whether they use these tools successfully depends on how their parents teach them to use these strategies (Fraiberg, 1959). In literature on effective ways to overcome fear in children it is consistently advised not to deny children's fears. When a child wakes up at night because there are monsters in his or her room that want to eat him or her, it is unwise to say: "That is silly, monsters don't exist." For young children, fantasies and dreams are often close to reality. If a child dreams about a monster, the monster really is there. In many cases denying therefore has a contradictory effect (Fraiberg, 1959; Sarafino, 1986).

Some adults believe that it is best to ignore the child's fear. They tell themselves that the fear is temporary and that in time the child will grow out of it. But according to Sarafino (1986) pretending fears do not exist is the same as "ignoring a child's 102 degree fever" (p. 80). In both cases, the child has a problem that might go away if nothing is done about it, but it might also get worse. However, it is not so bad to ignore a child's fear now and again—when it is a small fear that can be watched. But ordinary children's fears, such as fear of animals and monsters, have to be taken seriously when they surface.

Parents use various strategies to reassure their children when they are afraid of things they see in the media. Parents of young children often use physical strategies relatively often to comfort their child, such as putting him on their lap or giving him a cuddly toy. Physical strategies are most effective for young children because with young children there is often no point explaining that it is all make believe (Cantor, 2002). Parents of older children use cognitive strategies relatively often, such as explaining that the things the children see is make believe. These strategies may at first lead to children temporarily believing that everything they see on television is made up, including documentaries and the news. This response is typical; it is the process whereby children gradually learn to distinguish between what is real and what is make believe in the media they view (Wright et al., 1994).

Comforting children in the case of violent *news* requires specific strategies, as many cognitive strategies that are used in fiction are not relevant to news. Violent news can upset children in two ways: first, by direct confrontation with news footage, and second, through empathy, whereby children indirectly take on the fear and concern of their parents regarding the news. Children regard their parents as powerful problem solvers who protect them from danger. When children see that their parents are anxious when watching the news, they sense that there is danger and can become frightened themselves.

When children become frightened from watching violent news footage, parents often reassure them by saying that the perpetrator is sick or not well, and by assuring them that the danger in question cannot happen to them at home or in the area (Valkenburg, Walma van der Molen, & Peeters, 2001). If these strategies are not relevant, for example, because the danger is or can come nearby, it is recommended to be very careful about watching news on television, avoid expressing one's worries too much in the presence of the children, always respond to questions that children may have, and divert the children's attention by focusing on some positive aspects of the incident, such as the heroic role of the aid workers.

CONCLUSION

This chapter has shown that most children are at times so scared of something they have seen in the media that they remain afraid afterward. It has also shown that, for most children, this fear disappears after several hours or days. However, for approximately 10% to 12% of young viewers, the fear that a movie or television program evokes is much more serious. They remain frightened for weeks and sometimes months to years because of one terrifying scene. For them, that particular evening of channel hopping to the wrong movie has had some major consequences in their everyday life. Lack of sleep, not wanting to use the shower, and no longer daring to swim in the sea are examples revealed by our various studies.

Not only does news and entertainment designed for adults contain frightening elements for children, but so does children's entertainment. Much of this kind of entertainment is marketed as family movies, but they are not really for young children. These kinds of movies are only suitable for children who are able to reassure themselves by reasoning that what they see is "only make believe." As was shown, children younger than 7 are not able to do this very well. It is therefore important for adults to realize that even when an adult watches certain family movies together with a child, such movies can still intensely frighten young children.

5

Children and Advertising

The effect of advertising on children has always provoked strong feelings and contradictory opinions. This chapter provides insight into the current state of the empirical research on this topic. Consisting of four sections, the first examines some general aspects of children's consumer behavior. It begins with the question of why children have become an interesting niche market in the past decades. It also discusses the development of children's brand awareness and their growing influence on family purchases. The second section reviews some important effects of advertising on children. It will concentrate on some important intended (e.g., brand preferences) and unintended effects of advertising (e.g., materialism, parent–child conflict). The third section reviews a number of characteristics of advertising that may increase its effects on children, such as repetition of commercials, celebrity endorsement, and the use of premiums. The final section examines which children are most susceptible to the various effects of advertising. Research has shown, for example, that younger children are more vulnerable to certain advertising effects than older children. This section explains why various subgroups of children differ in their reactions to advertising.

CHILDREN, FAMILIES, AND CONSUMER BEHAVIOR

Over the past two decades, marketers of toys and children's products have developed a diverse spectrum of strategies to reach the child consumer. One important explanation for the increased interest in children is that the marketing world has discovered that children do not represent one, but three different markets. First, children form a primary market. In most western countries, children have become an attractive niche market, a distinct client group that has sufficient financial means and a need for specific products. Today's children have considerable amounts of money to spend on needs and wants of their own, which qualify them as a significant primary market (McNeal, 1992).

Children also form two other markets, namely an influence market and a future market. Various studies have shown that children have considerable influence on family purchases. Not only do they give direction to the selection of food and snacks, they also have a say in the choice of restaurant or the make of the new car. Finally, research has shown that adults often remain loyal to the brands they liked when they were children. Manufacturers who influence the brand attitudes of children therefore have a considerable chance that these favorable attitudes will last into adulthood (McNeal, 1992).

The increased economic power and influence on family purchases of today's children can be explained by various sociological changes in the 1970s and 1980s. As discussed in chapter 1, parents have higher incomes and better educational levels than ever before. In addition, they have fewer children and have them at a later age. There are more divorced parents, single–parent families, and dual working-parent families (McNeal, 1992). These factors all contribute to the fact that parents indulge their children's whims more often, tend to feel guilty more often, and do more to ensure that their children want for nothing (McNeal, 1999).

The Commercial Media Environment of Children

The fact that children have been discovered as three markets in one has major consequences for the commercial environment of children. Supermarkets and department stores, for example, invest more time and money than ever before in a child friendly layout by creating separate play areas, by offering children premiums, or simply by adopting brands in their range that children know well through advertising. It is also known that supermarkets intentionally put certain products and brands at a child's eye-level so that children can better see and reach them. This makes it more likely that the child would want to return to the store and encourage their parents to do so (McNeal, 1999).

The commercial media environment of children has also changed a great deal. First, the amount of television advertising aimed at young children has increased considerably. At present, there is more advertising aimed at young children than at teenagers (Buijzen & Valkenburg, 2000b). In addition to advertising, marketers of children's products increasingly utilize other, less obvious marketing practices that usually create less irritation among parents and adults. Sponsoring television programs, for example, has made large advances over the last decade. Sponsorship takes various forms. Sometimes it involves product placement. The frequent drinking of Coca-Cola in some comedies or soaps is an example of this. On occasion, the entire program is produced by the advertiser, whereby products of the advertiser are shown during the program in all sorts of ways (Neijens, 2000).

The increased trend toward the sponsoring of television programs has gone hand in hand with the proliferation of commercial television channels specifically geared toward children. Nowadays these commercial children's channels are, in contrast to the past, quite lucrative. There are various reasons for this. First, these channels concentrate primarily on cartoons and animation films, which with the new digital design systems can be produced more quickly and cheaply than before. Second, it is easier to sell these programs abroad than programs with real actors, because the characters (often animals or fantasy figures) are less dependent on culture, and can be dubbed much more easily. Finally, cartoons and animation programs are well suited to the merchandising of toys and products.

Merchandising through children's programs has until recently not attracted much criticism. Films and television series such as *Mickey Mouse* and *Sesame Street* have for a long time been connected with merchandising. Criticism was first voiced once cartoon and animation films began to be made primarily with the objective of earning money through merchandising. Children's programs, which are produced solely for merchandising of toys and products, are sometimes called program-length commercials. Examples of program-length commercials are the *Ninja Turtles*, *Power Rangers*, *Pokémon*, and *Teletubbies*. These entertainment programs, which are in fact commercials, are often not seen as such by either children or adults. The criticism directed at these programs has to do with the fact that governments or self-regulatory bodies are neglecting their responsibility of regulating these kinds of programs (Buckingham, 2000).

Another trend in the commercial media environment of children is that television programs, films, printed media, computer games, and the Internet are converged increasingly in relation to the marketing of toys and children's products. Take Pokémon, for example. Not only is there a Pokémon television series, there are also Pokémon films, Pokémon video games, and numerous Pokémon Internet sites. On top of all this, there are also Pokémon cards, toys, and many other accessories. Television commercials frequently direct children to Web sites of the children's program or product, where they can see, try out, and order the merchandized products.

Finally, the Internet provides advertisers with extra opportunities to expand their marketing practices aimed at children (Montgommery, 2000). Advertisers increasingly use the Internet to collect information on surfing visitors. They use this information to get to know their target group better and to more effectively gear their products to the wishes of this target group. In contrast to other media, the Internet allows advertisers to link their market research to advertising. This is clearly a questionable practice when children are involved. Studies have shown that children tend to freely give personal information via the Internet. In a study conducted by Turow and Nir (2000) American children from the ages of 10 to 16 were asked if they were willing to give their name, address, and information on what they liked and disliked in exchange for a free gift. Some 23% of the children said they were prepared to do so. At the end of the 1990s it was such common practice to collect information on children through the Internet, that in 1998 special legislation was introduced, the Children's Online Privacy Protection Act (COPPA). The purpose of this Act is to regulate the family-related information that children are asked to give. Since this Act came into effect in 2000, it is no longer permitted to ask children under the age of 13 personal information via the Internet without the consent of their parents. The following chapter will take a closer look at the COPPA and the commercial Internet environment of children.

Development of Children's Consumer Behavior

Children's consumer behavior has often been studied within the theoretical paradigm of consumer socialization. Consumer socialization is a rather effortless process by which children learn the skills, knowledge, and attitudes necessary to function as consumers. Although there is no single definition of a consumer, most definitions that have been employed seem to entail similar characteristics. A consumer is able to (a) feel and express wants and preferences; (b) search to fulfill these wants and preferences; (c) make a choice and a purchase; and (d) evaluate the product and its alternatives. Do children meet these criteria, and if so, at what age? I try to answer these questions in the following.

Feeling and Expressing Wants and Preferences. Initially the development of the consumer behavior of children occurs primarily via the interaction between parents, television advertising, and shops. As shown in chapter 2, even from the moment of their birth, children have particular preferences for tastes, colors, and sounds. From this moment, they also begin to communicate their wants and preferences to their parents. However, the initial expression of wants and preferences is primarily reactive: The child indicates when the stimulus offered is pleasant or unpleasant.

Searching to Fulfill Wants and Preferences. Once children reach 2 years of age, they begin to express their wants and preferences more actively. During this period, children discover that they have their own will and begin to experiment with this. Children now begin to actively ask for products that they like. This happens particularly when the products are in their direct vicinity, for example in the shop or on television. Our observation study, discussed in chapter 1, revealed that 16% of the toddlers and preschool children spontaneously asked for one or more products (candies, toys) during a 40-minute video with commercials and children's programs. A number of the reactions of the children are given in the following. The children from the ages of 2 to 3 asked particularly for food, whereas the 3- to 5-year-olds asked for food and toys.

> Boy (26 months) sees the Cookie Monster in *Sesame Street* eat a cookie: "Cookie?"
> Boy (33 months) sees the Teletubbies eat toast: "I want cookies!"
> Boy (44 months) sees a *Winnie the Pooh* commercial: "I want that, that one!!!"
> Boy (56 months.) sees Nintendo commercial: "I want all three of them!"
> Girl (56 months) sees Barbie commercial: "She has long hair, I want that one!"

Children can sometimes be very persistent when asking for something. This can lead to trying situations for parents, for example when they are with their children in a supermarket or toy shop. In one of our studies, 41% of parents of children of 2 years admitted to sometimes having conflicts with their children during shopping (Valkenburg & Cantor, 2001). This percentage rose sharply for the age group 2 to 5. With children of 3, some 59% of parents had at some time a conflict, and with children of 5 years of age this percentage rose to 70% of parents. Strikingly, the number of shopping conflicts began to decrease as of 6 years of age. These results are in line with previous studies that revealed that the parent–child conflict situations in the store showed a curvilinear pattern (first an increase and then a decrease; Isler, Popper, & Ward, 1987; Valkenburg & Cantor, 2001).

Why do store conflicts increase during the toddler and preschool phase, and why do they decrease again between the ages of 6 and 8? First, children of 5 to 6 years of age become better able to delay gratifications. Children younger than 6 have very few strategies for resisting temptations. If they see something attractive, they focus all their attention on the enticing aspects of this stimulus and find it very difficult to resist. Parents can try to divert their children's attention away from the temptation, but it is only when children reach 5 or 6 years of age that they are able to independently use techniques to delay gratification (Mischel & Ebbeson, 1970; Mischel & Mischel, 1983).

The decrease in store conflicts also has to do with the growing ability of children to apply sophisticated persuasion techniques. Very young children quite often ask and whine as well as show anger in order to persuade their parents. In contrast, older children tend to use more sophisticated persuasion techniques, such as negotiation, argumentation, soft-soaping, arousing sympathy, and even white lies (Williams & Burns, 2000). It is assumed that the persuasion techniques of children originate in the terrible twos, the phase in which 2-year-old children say practically nothing other than "no" and display explicit disobedient behavior. This disobedience is temporary, because children quickly realize that open forms of resistance are less effective. Although moaning, screaming, and anger are still relatively common in 3-year-olds, children of this age are already quite able to come up with compromises, alternative suggestions, and excuses for things that they do not want to do. Children soon realize that they can also use this type of strategy for things that they do want to do or have. This explains why parent–child conflicts decrease as of 6 or 7 years of age.

Making a Choice and a Purchase.   As of 5 years of age, children begin to make purchases independently. The process of choosing and paying for products in the shop initially takes place with the parents there. As Table 5.1 shows, three fourths of 5-year-old children have already bought something themselves with the parents present, whereas one fifth have bought things fairly regularly without their parents there. These percentages increase rapidly as the children grow older. By the time they reach 8 years of age the majority of children have bought something without their parents. At this age about one half of the children already go to the store regularly to buy things on their own. This is usually a nearby shop or supermarket at a safe walking distance (Valkenburg, 1999).

Evaluating Products and Their Alternatives.   In order to be able to evaluate products and compare them with alternatives, children need to have the ability to critically evaluate products on suitability and quality. Chapter 2 of this book shows that preschool school children and young primary school children scarcely have this ability. Due to their difficulty focusing on more than one aspect of a stimulus, they find it hard to look at the various details of a product at one go. Young children are not able to focus their attention on the various aspects or dimensions of a person or product, which is an important aspect of being able to form a good evaluation.

TABLE 5.1
Has Your Child Ever Bought Anything Independently?

Age of Child (in Years)	With You There (% Yes)	Without You There (% Yes)
4	54	2
5	74	21
6	79	18
7	81	35
8	83	48

Note.   Adapted from Valkenburg, 1999.

The critical ability of children develops rapidly after around 8 years of age. As of that age, every product that they look at is studied in detail and compared with other products. When a child of 8 gets a new pair of sport shoes, each part of the shoe, from the laces to the logo, is carefully examined and compared to the features of other shoes. These older children are also very critical of media products, for example whether they do look exciting, fun or trendy. As of 8 years of age, children begin to realize that commercials are made to entice them into buying products. Then these commercials also no longer escape their critical examination. In contrast to younger children, who primarily see commercials as entertainment, children of this age can be very skeptical about commercials (Young, 1990).

Children around 12 years of age have all the characteristics of a consumer. They can (a) express their wants and preferences (from birth), (b) take actions to satisfy their wants and preferences (as of 2 years of age), (c) make a choice and purchase (as of 5 years of age), and (d) critically evaluate a product and compare with alternatives (as of 8 years of age). Although, of course, the consumer behavior of children continues to develop during adolescence, by age 12, children have become acquainted with all aspects of their consumer behavior, at least in a rudimentary form (Valkenburg & Cantor, 2001).

Influence of Children on Family Purchases

At the outset of this chapter, it was suggested that children have a growing influence on family purchasing behavior and that this is one of the reasons why children have become interesting from a commercial point of view. According to McNeal (1999) the influence of children on family purchasing has been increasing steadily since the 1970s, but since the 1980s it has grown dramatically. In the 1990s alone, according to McNeal, the influence of children on family purchases has increased by 15%.

Why has the influence of children on family shopping increased so considerably over the past two decades? The reasons for this have already been mentioned earlier in this chapter: Parents have larger incomes, while families are growing smaller. There are more single-parent families and research has shown that children from these families are more involved in purchase decisions (Mangleburg, 1990). Parents are having children at a later age, and by the time the children arrive they are so desired that they receive a great deal of attention. The number of dual-working parents has also increased. These parents often feel that they have less time for the children than they would like and frequently compensate for their guilt feelings with material things. Finally, in most western countries there is a shift from an authoritarian style of upbringing to a more democratic style, in which great value is placed on the opinion, individuality, and involvement of the child.

Children seem to exert influence on their parents in two ways, direct and indirect. Children exert direct influence when they actively ask for or demand a product and give hints and recommendations whether asked or not. Indirect or passive influence is the situation in which parents take account of the wants and preferences of their children when shopping (Mangleburg, 1990; McNeal, 1999; Williams & Burns, 2000). According to McNeal many parents have a list in their head of the favorite brands of their children, which they take into account when shopping.

Various studies have attempted to give an insight into the influence of children on purchase decisions. A study by Galst and White (1976) revealed that children between the ages of 4 and 6 who go along with their parents to a supermarket, on average make 12 spontaneous requests to their parents to buy certain products. This is approximately one request every 2½ minutes. This number does not include the recommendations that these children made at the request of their parents. Sometimes parents gave their children a choice of two or more alternatives. These recommendations at the request of the parents occurred on average three times per supermarket visit.

Children start asking for products in the supermarket at an early age. Holden (1983) followed a number of mothers with their 2-year-old children while they were shopping. During a supermarket visit lasting 25 minutes, the 2-year-olds indicated an average of 18 times that they wanted a particular product. In 81% of the cases they did this by actually asking for the products. In the other cases they made it clear that they wanted something by, for example, standing up in the shopping cart, pointing at a product, or by grabbing hold of the product from the shopping cart. Last, a study by McNeal (1999) revealed that children of 4 to 12 years of age make an average of five purchase requests every day. When on vacation trips this number doubles to 10 requests per day.

What types of products do children ask for most often? Children ask for products that they consume themselves or in which they have a special interest, such as toys or products that come with a premium. The requests that children make to their parents change as they get older. Children up to the age of around 7 primarily ask for candies, toys, and snacks. Children from around 9 to 12 years of age mainly ask for clothes, sweets, and sport items (Isler et al., 1987).

The number of requests children make, however, says little about the influence they have on family purchases. To establish children's influence, it is necessary to know how often parents yield to the requests of their children. Various studies have shown that parents of 2-year-olds yield to 14% of children's purchase requests. When children are between the ages of 4 and 12, parents give in to 50% of children's requests. These percentages are higher if parents' delayed compliance is taken into account. Parents do not always yield immediately to the requests of their children; they can take some time in doing so (Atkin, 1978; Holden, 1983; Isler et al., 1987; Ward & Wackman, 1972).

The number of requests for products decreases when children reach about 7 years of age. This does not mean, however, that the influence children have on family purchases also decreases. On the contrary, various studies have shown that children actually have more influence on family purchases as they grow older (Mangleburg, 1990). An explanation of this somewhat paradoxical situation (fewer requests, yet more influence) is that older children exert more indirect or passive influence on their parents than do younger children. This phenomenon, known in the literature as *passive dictation*, refers to the situation in which parents automatically buy their children's favorite brands because they are familiar with these brands and wish to please their children (McNeal, 1999; Williams & Burns, 2000).

Many market researchers have tried to estimate children's relative influence on family purchases. This has been difficult because it is not easy to distinguish between the direct and indirect influence of children but also because both influences are difficult to quantify. Yet, some researchers have attempted to specify children's relative influence in percentages, and their estimates seem to be quite consistent. A study carried out by Hall, Shaw, Johnson, and Oppenheim (1995) investigated the relative influence of 5- to 18-year-olds on the purchase of 10 products, including computer games, vacation destinations, jeans, and the car. The relative influence on the purchase of all these products together was 30%. In other words, in the purchase of these 10 products the children had an average of 30% say in the purchase and parents 70%. The influence of children, however, varied strongly by product. Their influence was the highest for the purchase of video games, namely 73%. Vacation destinations were determined for 36% by the children. The choice of jeans was determined for 47%, and the choice of the car for 10% by the children.

McNeal (1999) also attempted to establish the influence of children on the purchase of 75 products. The average influence of children on all these 75 products together was 28%, a figure close to that of Hall et al. (1995). In addition, McNeal found a great variation in the relative influence for each product. The children exerted the greatest influence on products that were intended for themselves, such as toys, clothes, candies, and children's cosmetics (70% to 80%). They also had a large influence on things that were relevant to them, such as theme parks (45%), the choice of restaurant (30%) and educational software (50%). The smallest degree of influence that children had was on things that bore little relevance to them, such as cars (8%) and mineral water (9%).

The influence of children on family purchases varies not only by product. Many other factors play a role. As explained earlier, various studies have shown that as children grow older they exert more influence. In addition, children from families with a high income and from single-parent families have more influence. Finally, the style of upbringing of the parents seems to have an effect. Children from parents who have a more authoritarian style of upbringing have less influence than children from permissive and democratic parents (Mangleburg, 1990).

Development of Brand Awareness and Brand Preferences

At the beginning of this chapter, it was suggested that children form an important future market because once they are adults they tend to show a high degree of loyalty to the brands they liked and were familiar with when younger. To understand the phenomenon of brand loyalty it is important to comprehend how brand awareness and brand preferences develop in childhood. Brand awareness is the active or passive knowledge of a particular brand. Children show brand preference if they prefer a particular brand to others.

The literature regards both the brand awareness and the brand preferences of children as important predictors for future use of a product (Macklin, 1996; Mizerski, 1995). Both variables, however, are not necessarily related to one another. A study by Mizerski (1995) revealed that children were very aware of the cigarette brand Camel, but that their attitude toward this brand was not so favorable. On the contrary, the better they knew the brand, the more negative was their attitude toward Camel cigarettes.

Brand Awareness.   Children's brand awareness is often investigated by showing children brand logos or other stimuli (e.g., brand characters) and then measuring the extent to which they recognize or recall the relevant brands. Brand recognition is investigated by showing children brand logos or characters and then asking them to which brand or product the particular brand logo best fits. The children can choose from a number of options. In the case of brand recall, the children have to name the brand spontaneously while looking at the logos or characters.

Both brand recognition and brand recall are important when making purchase decisions. For a decision for a particular brand in the supermarket, only recognition is necessary because the various alternatives are alongside one another on the shelf. For a decision that has to be made at home, recall is necessary, as the various alternatives are not there at that time. In order to be able to function effectively as a consumer a child must learn to take both kinds of decisions, and must therefore be capable of brand awareness and brand recognition.

Brand *recognition* occurs earlier in the development of children than brand *recall*. A study by Fischer, Schwartz, Richards, Goldstein, and Rojas (1991), conducted among 3- to 6-year-olds revealed that 82% of the children recognized the McDonald's logo, in as far as they could combine it with a picture of a hamburger. In addition, 57% of the children could recognize the Nike logo, and some 52% knew that Joe Camel was associated with a picture of a packet of

Camel cigarettes. These findings are confirmed in a study by Mizerski (1995) in which 70% of 3-year-olds recognized the Disney logo and 25% the logo of Camel cigarettes.

So it seems that preschool children already have a strong ability to recognize brand logos. But are they also capable of recalling brands? After all, brand recall is a process that requires greater cognitive efforts than brand recognition. For brand recognition, children only have to choose from different options. Brand recall, on the other hand, requires that children deliberately search for relevant information in their memory.

To find out at what age children are capable of recalling brand logos, we surveyed 60 children from 5 to 9 years of age. Each child was individually shown 10 brand logos, including the logos of McDonalds hamburgers, Nike sportswear, Pepsi soft drink, Mercedes cars, and Shell Oil Company. For each logo, we asked the children if they could give the brand name. A total of 100% of the 5-year-olds could recall the brand name associated with the McDonald's logo. However, for the rest of the logos none of the 5-year-olds could spontaneously mention the brand name. Of the 6-year-olds, 58% could mention the brand name associated with the Nike logo. For brands that were not so relevant to children, such as Mercedes, more than one half of the 6-year-olds could recall the correct brand name. The brand recall of children increased considerably among children from the ages 5 to 9. Whereas the 5-year-olds could only name 1 out of 10 brand names, the 9-year-olds could do this for six out of the ten logos (Valkenburg & Van Wijnbergen, 2002).

Brand Preferences.   Although children tend to make their first purchase around 4 and 5 years of age, long before that time they have developed very specific preferences for certain brands. The study by Fischer et al. (1991) mentioned in the previous section demonstrated that approximately two thirds of children between the ages of 3 and 6 *often* or *almost always* ask their parents for specific brands. An experimental study by Hite and Hite (1995) revealed that children of 2 years of age prefer a peanut butter brand that was heavily advertised to the same peanut butter that was packaged as an unknown brand. The well-known peanut butter brand was also considered much tastier than the same peanut butter packaged as an unknown brand.

These studies clearly show that children develop brand preferences at an early age. However, it is not clear how these preferences develop as children grow older. Some authors claim that children's brand preferences change a lot in early childhood, but once children reach adolescence their preferences become relatively stable. A study by Middelmann and Melzer (1984) found that more than one half of 30-year-olds still use the brands they used when they were 16. This applied to products such as chocolate, jeans, coffee, mail-order companies, cosmetics, toiletries, and washing powder. Another study, however, indicated that this brand loyalty after adolescence certainly does not hold for all products. Moschis and Moore (1981) demonstrated, for example, that the preferences for some types of products and brands (e.g., soft drinks) were formed particularly in childhood, whereas the preferences for other products and brands developed during or after adolescence and were less stable than marketers would like.

ADVERTISING EFFECTS

The effects of advertising can generally be divided into two types: *intended* and *unintended effects*. Intended effects include the effects that advertisers wish to achieve with their advertisements. They may wish, for example, to influence children's brand awareness, brand preferences, and purchase requests. Unintended effects include the often undesired side effects of advertising. For example, it is sometimes asserted that advertising makes children materialistic and dissatisfied, and that it leads to unnecessary family conflict. In the next sections, I review the academic research into the most important intended and unintended effects of advertising.

Intended Effects

In the past three decades, approximately 50 academic studies have been published on the intended effects of advertising on children. This is not much when you consider that the effects of media violence on aggression has been the subject of several hundred studies. These studies can be roughly divided into three categories: studies into the effect of advertising on (1) brand awareness, (2) brand attitudes and brand preferences, and (3) purchase requests of children.

Influence of Advertising on Brand Awareness

The relationship between advertising and children's brand awareness has been studied in two ways. There is correlational research, in which the relation between the frequency that children watch television and their brand awareness is determined. There is also experimental research, in which children are shown one or more commercials, after which their brand awareness is determined.

Correlational Research.   Correlational research has been carried out into the brand recognition and the brand recall of children. In the studies into brand recognition children were shown a series of brand logos or brand characters, and were asked how often they watched television. In all these studies it was found that children who watched a great deal of television could recognize more brand logos or brand characters (Derscheid, Kwon, & Fang, 1996; Fischer et al., 1991; Goldberg, 1990).

The correlational research into the brand *recall* of children has come up with less clear results. In a study by Ward, Wackman, and Wartella (1977), children of 4 to 12 years of age were asked to name as many brands as possible from a particular product group. Although most products named were those that were advertised regularly on television, the relationship between watching television and brand recall was not significant. This nonsignificant effect of advertising on brand recall was confirmed in two other studies focusing on children between 4 and 14 years (Atkin, 1975d; Ward & Wackman, 1971). It must be noted, however, that when older adolescents (15- to 18-year-olds) are investigated, advertising does have a significant positive influence on brand recall (Ward & Wackman, 1971).

Experimental Research. In all experimental studies into the influence of advertising on brand recognition and brand recall, children were shown one or more commercials, after which the effect on their brand awareness was determined. As in the case of the correlational studies, the commercials had a considerable effect on the brand recognition of the children (Goldberg, 1990; Gorn & Florsheim, 1985; Gorn & Goldberg, 1980; Macklin, 1983). In a study by Macklin (1983), for example, four and five-year-old children were shown three commercials, one of which was for a cereal brand. After seeing just one commercial, 61% of the 4-year-olds and 65% of the 5-year-olds could recognize the cereal brand.

As is the case in the correlational studies, the experimental studies revealed that the brand recall of young children was affected less by advertising (Macklin, 1983; Macklin, 1994). However, again this nonsignificant advertising effect did not hold for older adolescents. A study by Dubow (1995), among 13- to 17-year-olds, demonstrated that television advertising had a large effect on their brand recall, even greater than its effect on adults.

Conclusion. Both the correlational research and experimental research shows that the influence of advertising on the brand recall of children is smaller than its influence on their brand recognition. There are various explanations for this. First, recalling things requires greater cognitive efforts than recognition. Recalling something requires a mental journey to a particular information unit in memory and then, in a second step, an evaluation whether the activated information unit is the correct one. In the case of recognition memory, only the second step is necessary. Most recall tasks, particularly those in which children have to come up with the brand name themselves, are probably too difficult for young children and are perhaps so difficult that advertising has little or no effect on their brand recall.

Another explanation for the finding that advertising has more effect on the brand recognition of older children than that of younger children is that older children possess better strategies to aid their memory, such as rehearsal, categorization, visualization of particular words, and mnemonics (e.g., Roy G. Biv for the colors of the rainbow). As of 7 years of age, children use these sorts of strategies increasingly often, thereby helping to increase their recall memory.

A final and perhaps the most important explanation for the finding that advertising has more effect on older children's brand recall is that older children have a greater knowledge than younger children. Recall studies have suggested that new information is best remembered when it is related to existing knowledge in the memory. Suppose that a child has to remember a new brand name, *Jumbo* for instance. For a young child *Jumbo* is a brand new word, for which an entirely new memory unit has to be created. An older child can relate the word *Jumbo* to already existing knowledge in memory, such as elephant, trunk, jungle, or airplane. This is the reason why it is easier for older children to remember new brand names than young children. This may also explain why the effect of advertising on the brand recall of older children is greater than that of younger children.

Influence of Advertising on Brand Attitude and Brand Preferences

The second type of research into the effects of advertising focuses on the question of whether advertising can ensure that children are given a positive attitude toward an advertised brand and whether they prefer certain brands to others. This research examines, for example, whether children under the influence of advertising like the advertised brand (better), whether their desire for the brand is aroused, or whether they would choose advertised brands in preference to others.

Before I discuss the advertising-brand attitude studies, I want to deal with the question of whether it is theoretically plausible that children like certain brands better under the influence of advertising. After all, every communication scholar knows that attitudes in general, and brand attitudes in particular, are difficult to influence, or at least more difficult than brand awareness. The hypothesis that exposure to advertising is sufficient to have a positive effect on brand attitudes and preferences may be based on a simplistic influence model. As became clear earlier in this book, even the youngest of children have distinct ideas on what they do and do not like. Their attitudes toward brands are determined by many factors, including their gender, cognitive level, temperament, media preferences, and their susceptibility to peer influence. All these factors determine their selective exposure and attention to media content and advertising, and, as a result, the effects of these media contents. If children are not interested in the content of a commercial, it is unlikely that their brand attitudes and preferences will be influenced by it. To influence children's brand attitudes, one likely needs more than just exposure to advertising.

Correlational Research.   Atkin (1975c) was one of the first to find that exposure to advertising was not enough on its own to influence the brand preferences of children. Atkin asked 755 children how often they had seen a certain commercial for a Snoopy pencil sharpener. He also asked them whether they liked the commercial and pencil sharpener. Initially he found a significant relation between advertising exposure and children's attitude toward the pencil sharpener. This significant relation, however, disappeared once children's attitudes toward the commercial were controlled. In other words, it did not make any difference whether children watched a commercial a few or many times, the crucial predictor was whether they liked the commercial.

More recent correlational research confirmed that children's brand preferences are heavily influenced by their preference for the specific commercial. Sometimes correlations of above $r = 0.70$ have been found between liking the commercial and liking the brand (e.g., Derbaix & Bree, 1997). A study by Moore and Lutz (2000) revealed that the relation between liking a commercial and liking a brand is greater for children younger than 8 years of age than for older children. According to the authors, this is because younger children are less critical of advertisements than older children.

Experimental Research.   The effect of advertising on the brand attitude of children has also been investigated in various experimental studies. Some studies focused on sweets, ice cream, or cereals; others on toys; and still others on personal-care products, such as anti-acne products or lipstick. Most studies showed children one or more commercials and then asked them how much they liked the advertised product.

In a study by Atkin (1975b) one half of a group of 7- to 10-year-olds were shown a video into which a commercial for the anti-acne product Clearasil was edited. The other half of the children were not shown this commercial. At the end of the video, both groups of children were asked what they thought of Clearasil. The children who had seen the Clearasil commercial had a more positive brand attitude toward it than those who had not seen it. The effect was greater for girls and held only for those children who were not familiar with the commercial. The finding that girls' brand attitudes in particular were affected might be because an anti-acne product is more relevant to girls of this age who reach puberty earlier than boys. The finding that only children who were unfamiliar with the commercial were affected in their attitudes might be explained by the fact that the children who did not know the commercial had had relatively less opportunity to develop critical thoughts and counterarguments against the claims presented in the commercial.

In a study by Gorn and Goldberg (1977) boys of 8 to 10 years of age were shown a cartoon. The study consisted of four experimental groups. In the first group, one commercial for a new brand of toy was shown during the cartoon. In two other groups, either two or three commercials were shown during the cartoon. A control group was not shown any commercials. The brand attitude of those who had seen the commercial was significantly higher than that of those who had not seen the commercial. It made no difference whether the boys had seen the commercial once, twice, or three times.

Conclusion. Both the correlational and experimental studies show that advertising can affect children's brand attitudes although it does not necessarily have to happen. When a small effect is found at the aggregate level (for all children together), there may be a larger, smaller, or even no effect at all within certain subgroups. The effect of advertising on the brand attitude and preferences of children is determined by many factors, including the age of the child, the familiarity with the brand, the interest in the advertised brand or product, and the child's liking of the commercial.

Influence of Advertising on Purchase Requests

Studies into the effects of advertising on children's request behavior have consistently demonstrated that children who often watch commercial television ask their parents for products more often (e.g., Atkin, 1975c; Buijzen & Valkenburg, 2000a, 2003b; Galst & White, 1976; Robertson & Rossiter, 1976; Robertson, Ward, Gatignon, & Klees, 1989).

The approximate correlations in the different correlational studies vary from $r = 0.18$ (Isler et al., 1987) to $r = 0.41$ (Atkin, 1975d). In the majority of studies the reported correlations were around $r = 0.30$. If we interpret this correlation coefficient using the conversion method of Rosenthal and Rubin (1982) discussed in chapter 3, it seems that children who watch commercial television at an above median level have on average a chance of 65% of asking for advertised products, whereas children of below median level have on average a chance of 35% of asking for products. Such a difference in the request behavior between light and heavy watchers of commercial television is, of course, very important to advertisers and marketers—certainly important enough to invest large amounts of money in extensive advertising campaigns for children's products.

Unintended Effects

Research into the unintended effects of advertising has focused on the question of whether advertising (a) makes children materialistic, (b) stimulates family conflicts, and (c) makes children unhappy.

Does Exposure to Advertising Lead to Materialism?

A number of researchers have suggested that advertising makes children materialistic. Several studies have examined whether this is indeed the case. In the correlational studies that have been carried out, materialism has been investigated by asking children to respond to various statements, such as "It is true than money can make you happy" and: "It is my dream to be able to have expensive things." With one exception (Ward & Wackman, 1971), all correlational studies found positive relations between the viewing frequency of commercial television and the materialistic attitude of children and adolescents. The correlations vary between $r = 0.13$ (Atkin, 1975c) and $r = 0.32$ (Moshis & Moore, 1982). The experimental studies, too, show that advertising has an effect on the materialistic attitudes of children (Goldberg & Gorn, 1978; Greenberg & Brand, 1993). However, the longitudinal study by Moschis and Moore (1982), suggests that advertising only stimulates materialism in children from families where consumer matters are not discussed (see Buijzen & Valkenburg, 2003a).

Does Advertising Increase Parent–Child Conflict?

A number of authors have suggested that advertising contributes to conflicts between parents and children. The underlying idea here is that advertising encourages children to ask for the advertised product. Because parents naturally do not want to comply with all these product requests, they have to say "no" to their children more often. As a result, the chance of conflicts between the parent and child increases.

The question of whether advertising exposure increases the number of product requests has already been discussed. This is an intended advertising effect, and research shows that this effect exists. But do these increased product requests lead to more parent–child conflicts? The relationship between purchase requests and family conflict has been investigated in three correlational studies. These studies all found a significant and high positive correlation between the number of purchase requests and parent–child conflicts (Atkin, 1975c, 1975d; Robertson et al., 1989).

An experiment conducted by Goldberg and Gorn (1978) also suggests that advertising can stimulate parent–child conflict. In this study, one half of a group of 4- and 5-year-olds were shown a children's program into which a commercial for an appealing toy was edited. The other half of the group was not shown this commercial. At the end, all children were asked whether they preferred to have a tennis ball or the advertised toy. It was added that their mothers preferred them to have the tennis ball. Children who had seen the commercial went against the wishes of their mothers more often (45.8%) than those children who had not seen the commercial (21.3%).

Does Advertising Lead to Dissatisfaction and Unhappiness?

Finally, some researchers believe that advertising makes children unhappy. Various hypotheses have been put forward with this claim. The first derives from the *social comparison theory*. It is assumed that advertising paints a world for children full of beautiful people and desirable products. If children watch too many commercials and compare them to their own situations, the contrast between the two worlds can make them unhappy. The few studies that investigated this hypothesis have focused on the effect of beautiful models in magazines on the self-perception of teenage girls and female students. These studies have produced mixed results. An experiment by Richins (1991) found that female students after seeing a printed advertisement with a beautiful female model felt less good about themselves. In a study by Martin and Kennedy (1993), no influence of advertising on the way the girls perceived their own looks was found.

Another hypothesis involves the manner in which children's toys and products are presented in commercials. By using certain camera techniques (e.g., close-ups, moving images of toys that do not themselves move), commercials can create high expectations among children about the actual performance and quality of the product. It is assumed that young children are not good at seeing through these techniques. If the product is a disappointment after purchase, children can become frustrated, disappointed, and unhappy. This hypothesis has been investigated only once. In a survey conducted among 253 6- to 11-year-old boys, a small negative relation was found between exposure to advertising and satisfaction with the product. This relation applied only to the youngest children in the sample (Robertson, Rossiter, & Ward, 1985). It is obvious that the research into the relation between advertising and feelings of unhappiness is too scarce to draw decisive conclusions (see Buijzen & Valkenburg, 2003a).

CHARACTERISTICS OF COMMERCIALS INFLUENCING EFFECTS

Some of the advertising-effects research has focused on the question of which characteristics of commercials increase their effectiveness. Six factors have been examined that can possibly increase one or more advertising effects. These are: (1) repetition of the commercial, (2) the use of peer-popularity appeal, (3) offering a premium, (4) celebrity endorsement, (5) host selling, and (6) the use of visual cues on the packaging of the advertised product.

Repetition

Repeating commercials has been shown to improve both children's brand recognition and their brand recall (Gorn & Goldberg, 1980; Macklin, 1994). However, there is probably no effect of repetition on their brand attitudes or preferences (Atkin, 1975a; Gorn & Goldberg, 1977), although an experiment by Gorn and Goldberg (1980) suggests that repetition affects children's brand attitudes if children are exposed to different commercials for the same brand. It is not known whether repetition of commercials increases children's purchase requests. It is also still an open question whether repetition stimulates one or more unintended advertising effects.

Peer-Popularity Appeal

Commercials for toys or other children's products often show two or more cheerful children together enjoying the advertised toy or product. These commercials employ the peer-popularity appeal. Earlier in this book it was shown that the effect of media increases when the observed models experience positive consequences for their behavior. The underlying mechanism here is observational learning (Bandura, 1986). In commercials that make use of the peer-popularity appeal, children are given the impression that they can feel as good and popular as the children in the commercial. It is assumed that this increases the effectiveness of advertising.

The effect of a peer-popularity appeal has been investigated by Loughlin and Desmond (1981). In this study, children were shown a commercial for an unknown toy, the Dancing man doll. One half of the children were shown a version with four happy, enthusiastic children playing with the Dancing man doll. The rest were shown a version in which only one child was playing with the toy (the control group). The children who had seen the peer-popularity commercial did not seem to want the advertised product any more than the children from the control group. In comparison to the control group, the children from the peer-popularity commercial did think that the commercial was more fun and that they would be more inclined to give the advertised product to a friend. The study of Loughlin and Desmond only investigated the effect of the peer popularity appeal on children's brand attitude. It is not known whether this appeal has a positive effect on their brand awareness and purchase intention. It is also not known whether the unintended effects of advertising are increased by this appeal.

Premiums

A premium is a gift that you receive for buying the advertised product. The use of premiums to induce sales to children probably began with Cracker Jack. Since then the American cereal industry became famous for using premiums (McNeal, 1992). Various studies have been carried out into the effect of commercials that use a premium. All these studies used cereal commercials. A study by Miller and Busch (1979) among 5- to 12-year-old children found that a premium increased children's brand preferences. In this study, the children who had seen a commercial with a premium chose the brand twice as much as those who had not seen this commercial. The premium commercial also stimulated children's brand recall, but this held only for 5- to 7-year-olds and not for older children.

Atkin (1975a) also found that a premium in a commercial increased children's desire for a cereal brand. However, this result applied only to 3- to 7-year-olds, and not for older children. Atkin did not find any effect on the purchase intention of children. Other studies did not reveal any significant effects of a premium for either brand awareness or for brand preference and request behavior (Heslop & Ryans, 1980; Shimp, Dyer, & Devita, 1976).

Celebrity Endorsement

The term *celebrity endorsement* refers to advertisements in which a well-known person sings the praises of a particular product. Celebrity endorsement has come about from the long-established view in social psychology that a trustworthy sender in the communication process can be more persuasive than an unknown sender (Hovland & Weiss, 1951). Celebrities attract attention to the advertisement and are seen by the public as interesting, authoritative, and credible. Additionally, many people, even adults, believe that celebrities praise the advertised brand because they have a genuine affection for the brand (rather than that they have been paid to do so). Such celebrities are often sports people, actors, or other personalities from the entertainment world (Atkin & Block, 1983). In many countries, it is forbidden to have celebrities promote products in advertisements aimed at children. Such celebrities have, after all, a special sort of authority, the use of which, in the case of advertisements aimed at children, is regarded as unethical.

Although the use of celebrities in endorsing products is seen as a successful strategy in the advertising world, there has been little academic research into its effect on children. Atkin and Block (1983) investigated the effect of using celebrities in alcohol advertisements on the brand attitude and purchase intention of adolescents between 13 and 17 years of age. The adolescents were shown three magazine advertisements in which the brands were endorsed either by a celebrity or by an unknown person. One advertisement for a brand of whisky featured either Kojak (Telly Savalas) or an unknown middle-aged man in the same sort of clothes and with a similar look. The adolescents did indeed think that the celebrities were more reliable, appealing, and competent than the unknown people. The adolescents who had seen the advertisements with the celebrities had a more positive attitude toward the advertised brand and they were more likely to buy the advertised brand.

In a study by Ross et al. (1981) conducted among boys between 8 and 14 years of age, the children were shown a commercial for a toy racing car, with either celebrity endorsement (a famous racer) or no endorsement. In this study the use of the celebrity was found to have no effect on the boys' brand attitude. However, it should be pointed out that the racing car commercials that were used in this study had been shown regularly on television at the time of the study. This is quite unusual in experimental studies into the effects of advertising, which normally use unknown commercials or ones that have not been used for a long time. The children's familiarity with the commercial could well have masked any experimental effects. After all, it is difficult to determine the effect of a single commercial in an experiment when the same commercial has been shown numerous times on television.

Host Selling

Host selling refers to a situation in which a character is featured in a television program and in the commercial slot before, during, or after that program. It is important to realize that the term *host* is interpreted quite broadly in the literature. A presenter does not necessarily have to be a person of flesh and blood. When a cartoon character appears in a commercial as well as the main program this is also considered to be host selling. Most studies have actually focused on the effect of these cartoon celebrities. Host selling has been banned in most countries because it is considered unethical to expose children, who often have difficulty distinguishing advertising from entertainment, to commercials that feature the same main character as the associated program.

The effects of host selling have been addressed in several studies. Atkin (1975a) has looked into the effect of host selling on the brand recall and the brand attitude of children of 3 to 10 years of age. As a host, Atkin used Fred Flintstone, a cartoon character who at the time was functioning as a brand character of a well-known cereal. Atkin showed two groups of children a commercial in which Fred Flintstone was praising the cereal brand. In one group, the commercial was incorporated in a Flintstones cartoon, and in another group in a Bugs Bunny cartoon. There was no difference in the brand recall of the children of the two experimental conditions. However, children in the host selling condition did have approximately 50% more desire for the cereal brand than the children in the control condition.

The results of Atkin (1975a) were confirmed by a study by Miller and Busch (1979), the only study in which a real-life presenter, Mr. Magic, was used to endorse a cereal brand. As was the case in Atkin's (1975a) study, the host-selling commercial did not lead to differences in brand awareness of 5- to 12-years-olds, although it did lead to differences in their brand preferences.

The remaining studies showed rather mixed results. In an experiment by Kunkel (1988) host selling only had an effect on the brand attitude and the request behavior of 7- and 8-year-old children. For 4- and 5-year-olds the endorsing celebrity, strangely enough, had the opposite effect. In these younger children, the host-selling commercial resulted in a more negative brand attitude and in less request behavior than the control commercial. Finally, in an experiment by Wilson and Weiss (1992) conducted among girls of four to eleven years of age no effect was found at all. However, this study used a commercial for a plastic doll (Beetlejuice doll) that was found later in the course of the study to be quite unpopular amongst the girls, which may explain this study's lack of finding significant effects of host selling.

Visual Cues on the Packaging of the Advertised Product.   Visual cues on the packaging that are directly related to the content of the commercials can stimulate children's brand awareness, brand attitude, and request behavior. This has been shown by two studies by Macklin (1994, 1996). In one of the studies children between the ages of 3 and 8 were shown five products of unknown brand names, for example a soft drink called *Night*. They were then asked to remember the brand name of the product. In one experimental condition, the memory of the children was stimulated by a visual cue in the form of a picture (in the case of the soft drink Night, a starry night). The control group did not receive any visual cues. The 3- to 5-year-olds who had received the visual cues remembered the brand name some 10 times better than the children in the control group. The 7- and 8-year-olds who had received the visual cues remembered the brand name approximately 1½ times better.

Another study by Macklin (1994) investigated the effect of a brand character on the packaging of a cereal brand. Children were first shown a commercial for a cereal brand called Jumpers. The commercial featured a frog, also called Jumpers. One half of the children were then shown a box of the cereal that had a picture of Jumpers the frog on it, while the other half was shown a box without the frog. It turned out that the packaging with the frog, in contrast to the box without, stimulated not only children's brand awareness, but also their brand attitude and request behavior.

CHILD CHARACTERISTICS INFLUENCING ADVERTISING EFFECTS

Brand Awareness

The effect of advertising on children's brand awareness (i.e., brand recall and recognition) is equal for boys and girls (Miller & Busch, 1979; Zuckerman, Ziegler, & Stevenson, 1978). However, its effect is not equal for different age groups. Although advertising has similar effects on younger and older children's brand *recognition*, its effect on brand *recall* is smaller for younger than for older children (Atkin, 1975a; Macklin, 1983; Stoneman & Brody, 1983).

This smaller effect is caught up by the time children reach 12 years of age. During adolescence, the effect of advertising on brand recall reaches a peak.

Brand Preferences

There are numerous factors that can influence the effect of advertising on children's brand preferences, including their gender, age, socioeconomic status, interest in the product or brand, and experience with the brand in question. However, little is known how these child characteristics determine advertising effects on brand preferences. The available research has concentrated only on the child's age as a moderating variable.

Various studies have shown that the effect of advertising on children's brand attitudes is greater for children under the age of 8 (Atkin, 1975a; Loughin & Desmond, 1981; Wilson & Weiss, 1992). It has also been found that the relationship between children's attitude toward the commercial and their brand attitude is greater for younger than older children. In other words, if younger children like a commercial, the chance that they will also like the advertised brand is greater than for older children (Moore & Lutz, 2000).

There are several explanations for why younger children are more receptive to advertising effects on brand attitudes. First, it is assumed that children only begin to be able to form and maintain stable attitudes once they reach about 8 years of age (Piaget, 1981). Children younger than 8 are, therefore, more easily swayed by an appealing commercial than older children, who are better able to relate and compare new information to their existing attitudes toward the advertised product or brand.

Another explanation for the relatively high receptivity of younger children is that younger children have less experience and knowledge that they can use when processing commercials. Because of this, they are less able to come up with critical thoughts and counterarguments when watching commercials, which inherently makes them more susceptible to persuasive information. This specific way of information processing of younger children has been called stimulus driven, whereas that of older children has been characterized as schema driven (Young, 1990).

A third explanation is that children of up to about 8-years-old are not capable of realizing the persuasive intent of advertising. In contrast to older children, they see advertising primarily as entertainment and are not yet able to critically evaluate its content. As discussed earlier, persuasive effects are generally greater when the source is perceived as credible. Because young children cannot see through many persuasive techniques, far more sources are considered as credible. This might be the reason why younger children are more easily convinced by attractive advertising claims than older children are.

Age and Skepticism Toward Advertising.   From about 8 years of age, children begin to become more critical and skeptical of advertising. This development reaches its peak at around 12 years of age (Boush, 2001). However, the fact that children become more skeptical of certain commercials does not mean to say that they are skeptical about all commercials. Riecken and Ugur (1990), for example, demonstrated that children can be very critical about some commercials (e.g., for detergents), but not at all in the case of others. Moreover, children's skepticism does not necessarily have to preclude their credulity. A study by Linn, de Benedictis, and Delucchi (1982) shows that adolescents who were highly critical about certain techniques used in commercials—for example comparative tests—often still believed the results of these tests.

The fact that older children are less susceptible to advertising effects on their brand attitude than younger children does not mean that the effects on older children are negligible. The assumption that knowledge and cognitive level are sufficient to neutralize advertising effects is based on an unsophisticated influence model. After all, commercials not only invoke cognitions but also emotions. And emotions are difficult to regulate with knowledge and reason. In fact, you may very well know that a film is unrealistic but you can still feel sad, frightened or happy when watching it. Similarly, you may know that your lover is cheating on you, but you may still want to continue the relation. This is also the case with the effects of advertising. Although a child may know that a commercial uses sophisticated persuasion strategies, a product can still be highly appealing.

How is it possible that children (and adults, for that matter) can be tempted by advertising when they know that they are being manipulated? The answer to this is similar to the story of the law of apparent reality as mentioned in chapter 4, which explained how and why viewers can experience emotions with fictitious media products. Advertising, just like fictitious entertainment, can be consumed in two ways. Viewers can suppress the development of skeptical thoughts, which would otherwise subdue their longing for the brand. Perhaps viewers do not mind occasionally being taken for a ride, especially if the commercial involves products or brands that are relevant to them personally. Older children and adults often realize that some advertisements exaggerate, but can still enjoy them or find them informative. However, viewers may also choose (consciously or subconsciously) to be skeptical. This can happen, for example, when commercials exaggerate their claims too much. This can also happen with brands in which the viewer has no interest or with which he or she has had negative experiences.

Purchase Requests

It is quite possible that certain characteristics of children, such as gender, age, and the socioeconomic status of the family, can influence the effect of advertising on purchase requests. However, very little research has investigated how these background factors influence advertising effects on the purchase requests of children. It is quite possible that for younger children there is a relatively greater direct relationship between watching commercials and request behavior. After all, younger children generally have more difficulty delaying gratification and diverting their attention from the tempting aspects of particular products than older children. Therefore, it is conceivable that advertising has a greater influence on the request behavior of younger than older children, but this has not been investigated.

Conclusion. The studies into the effect of advertising that have investigated background variables have focused only on the gender and age of the child. Gender has been found to exert no influence on the effect of advertising on brand awareness and brand preferences of children. The role of gender in the effect of advertising on children's request behavior has not been studied sufficiently to draw any conclusions. Age, however, does have an influence, although it differs for the various types of advertising effects. The studies that have investigated the effect of advertising on brand awareness have shown that age has a *positive effect*: the older the children, the greater the effect of advertising. However, with brand preferences, age has a *negative effect*: the older the child, the less the effect of advertising. However, this age difference shows up only when comparing children younger than 8 years of age with older children. The role that age plays in the effect of advertising on children's request behavior has not sufficiently been studied to come to any conclusions.

CHAPTER

6

Uses and Effects of Interactive Media

Children's use of interactive media has increased tremendously in the past few years. This chapter provides insight into the latest research on children, electronic games, and the Internet. Of the chapter's three sections, the first concentrates on the interactive media environment of children. It reveals a number of distinctive characteristics of children's entertainment Web sites and it reviews the various types of video and computer games that are currently available. The second section focuses on children's access to interactive media. It examines which children use the various types of interactive media and how this differs among boys and girls from differing age groups and backgrounds. The final section reviews a number of positive and negative effects of interactive media. It discusses the most important physical (e.g., epileptic seizures, Nintendonitis), cognitive (e.g., intelligence, eye-hand coordination), and social effects (e.g., family communication, friendship formation, aggression) of interactive media.

THE INTERACTIVE MEDIA ENVIRONMENT OF CHILDREN

This section first discusses characteristics and activities of commercial and non-commercial children's Web sites. Then, it describes the various types of video and computer games that are available both online and offline, and finally, it examines some specific trends in the interactive media environment of children.

Web Sites for Children

The number of Web sites specifically aimed at children has grown at a staggering rate over the past few years (Montgommery, 2000). These Web sites can generally be divided into three categories. There are the nonprofit sites that have been developed by the government, museums, libraries, and noncommercial broadcasting companies, which often combine education with entertainment. Then there are the commercial sites, which can be further divided into *media-based* and *product-based* sites. Media-based sites are the sites of commercial television channels, such as Fox Kids, Nickelodeon, and Cartoon Network. Product-related sites are the sites of toy companies and manufacturers of children's products, such as Mattel and Nintendo, most of which have Web sites for children (Montgommery, 2000).

Children's Web sites, regardless of whether they are commercial or not, resemble one another closely with regard to the activities they offer. Web games can be found on virtually all sites. It is often possible to chat, send digital cards, view films, and listen to or download music on these sites. On some Web sites you can enter competitions or send e-mails to celebrities. Some sites provide the possibility of Short Message Service (SMS) and Instant Messaging (IM). Some special game sites allow children to exchange messages about the progress of the game while they are playing. Many children's sites ask children to register if they are visiting for the first time. The children have to submit information such as their age, gender, address, and e-mail address. In most cases, parental consent is required before registering.

The preferred sites among children are the commercial sites. In a study by Henke (1999), 74% of the children named a commercial site as their favorite. In addition, Montgommery (2000) demonstrated that the majority of sites from the top 25 of popular children's sites have a commercial aim. These sites were from media conglomerates such as Nickelodeon, Disney, Fox, and Time Warner, and from toy manufacturers such as Nintendo, Lego, and Mattel. In our own research in the Netherlands, we found that Dutch children almost exclusively prefer to visit commercial sites, particularly the media-based ones (Fox Kids and Cartoon Network; Valkenburg & Buijzen, 2003).

Primary Goal of Commercial Web Sites:
Stimulating Brand Awareness and Brand Attitudes

Although Internet sites for children, until now, have seldom been profitable, practically all manufacturers of children's products and children's entertainment have created their own Web sites. The purpose of these sites, which have been referred to as *branded communities*, is two-fold. The primary goal is to familiarize children with brands drawing on the motto "love my community, love my brand" (Montgommery, 2000, p. 153).

The Internet provides a unique opportunity to stimulate children's brand awareness and brand attitudes. Children and young people, after all, are often the early adopters of new digital technologies. Although no advertiser of children's products would underestimate the value and effectiveness of television advertising to stimulate children's brand awareness, in marketing circles, it is well known that web advertising provides unique opportunities to reach the child market. In comparison to the Internet, television has fewer possibilities to familiarize children with brands, primarily offering only expensive commercials that last no more than 30 seconds. In contrast, on the Internet children can play for hours in a branded community where it is difficult to make a distinction between entertainment and advertising. Children often do not realize that they are visiting a site that has a commercial aim. This inability of children to make a distinction between entertainment and advertising is already a problem with television, although television commercials are placed in distinct advertising slots (Young, 1990). The study by Henke (1999) revealed that only 13% of the children from the ages of 9 to 11 realized that the aim of their favorite commercial site was advertising. By far the majority of children (74%) thought that their favorite site was there to entertain them.

Secondary Goal of Commercial Web Sites: Collecting Market Data

A second goal of commercial Web sites is to capitalize on the possibilities these children's sites offer for collecting market data. This occurs in various ways. First, children are asked for personal information (age, gender, address, e-mail address, etc.) when registering. However, on some sites, children are also regularly confronted with surveys, asking them for information such as their preferences regarding the content and activities of the site and the products they offer. The answers to these questions are used by advertisers to modify their Web site and products so that they can better meet the wishes of children.

Information on the users is also collected via cookies. A cookie is a piece of software stored in a text file that is transferred from a Web site onto the computer of a visitor. Cookies are made by the Web site operator and are installed automatically on the visitor's hard disk. Cookies inform the Web site as to which parts of the site have been visited and for how long. In this way they inform the Web site operator on the strengths and weaknesses of the site. Cookies can also be used to determine the profile of the various visitors, and can be used to collect market data that can be exchanged with other companies (Davidson, 1999).

The majority of entertainment sites make it no secret that they use the information they gather from registration surveys and cookies to optimize their sites, products, and brands. Their privacy policies in which this sort of information is stated are often placed on their site. These privacy rules may state, for example, that the site shares information obtained from visitors with other advertisers.

In 1996 the American Center for Media Education conducted a content analysis into the collection of personal data of children via the Web. This survey revealed that many of the children's sites used games, surveys and competitions to collect information on children. A year later, an analysis of children's Web sites commissioned by the Federal Trade Commission showed that 86% of the children's sites collected personal information from children (Montgommery, 2000).

In 1998, these research results gave rise to the Children's Online Privacy Protection Act (COPPA), which has already been mentioned in the previous chapter. Since the introduction of the COPPA, which became effective in April 2000, it is forbidden to use the Web to collect information on children younger than 13 years of age without parental consent. The most important sections of the COPPA, taken from http://www.ftc.gov/bcp/conline/pubs/buspubs/coppa.htm, are outlined in Table 6.1.

The question remains, however, whether the COPPA sufficiently hampers the collection of personal information via children's Web sites. In preparation for this chapter, I visited many children's sites, where I posed as a 12-year-old. My experience was that many children's sites still collected information on

TABLE 6.1

Most Important Sections of the COPPA (Children's Online Privacy Protection Act)[1]

1. All Web sites directed to children under 13 that collect personal information from children must comply with the Children's Online Privacy Protection Act.

2. A Web site operator must post a link to a notice of its information practices on the home page of its Web site or online service and at each area where it collects personal information from children.

3. The COPPA applies to individually identifiable information about a child that is collected online, such as full name, home address, e-mail address, telephone number or any other information that would allow someone to identify or contact the child. The COPPA also covers other types of information—for example, hobbies, interests and information collected through cookies or other types of tracking mechanisms.

4. Before collecting, using or disclosing personal information from a child, a Web site operator must obtain verifiable parental consent from the child's parent.

5. A Web site operator must notify a parent that it wishes to collect personal information from the child, that the parent's consent is required for the collection, use and disclosure of the information, and how the parent can provide consent.

6. At a parent's request, Website operators must disclose the general kinds of personal information they collect online from children (e.g., name, address, telephone number, hobbies), as well as the specific information collected from children who visit their sites.

[1]The entire rules and regulations of the COPPA are online available: www.ftc.gov/bcp/conline/pubs/buspubs/coppa.htm

children, via registration, surveys, or cookies. After visiting these children's sites, I found many cookies in my cookies folder, including those of Nintendo, Barbie, Fox Kids, and Cartoon Network. What is more, on the children's sites I was regularly asked survey questions, and at no time was permission "from my parents" asked.

European commercial sites regularly collect personal information from children, as well as information that, were the COPPA to be applied in Europe, would not be allowed to be collected. Fox Kids in the Netherlands, for example, rewards child visitors with bonus points (called brix) every time they complete a survey. These surveys ask the opinions of children on, for example, the Fox Kids Web site, mobile telephones, SMS, the brand of their favorite game computer, and the type of games they prefer. For each survey they complete they receive 50 to 200 brix. Once they have collected 35,000 brix they are allowed to choose a gift from the "Brix boutique." The privacy rules of Fox Kids state that the data from the children are used to improve their Web site and products and that the information is shared with other companies with which they do business. These companies could then approach these children directly with their products.

Different Types of Video and Computer Games

In the world of gamers, a clear distinction is made between video and computer games. Video games are played on a game console such as Playstation, X-Box, or Nintendo, which have to be connected to the television or be used as the handheld Nintendo's Game Boy. Computer games are played on a computer. The academic world rarely makes this distinction between these two types of games. Although the graphics of both types of games are of identical quality, there is an important difference in the use of both types of games. Boys between the ages of 2 to 13 play, for example, three to five times as many video games as girls of the same age, whereas there is hardly any difference between the genders when it comes to computer games (Roberts et al., 1999). In addition, children from families with lower incomes play relatively more video games than computer games, probably because a game console is cheaper than a computer (Roberts et al., 1999). Although video and computer games have an important characteristic in common, namely their interactivity, for the aforementioned reasons it is wise not to generalize the use of these two types of games. In this chapter, therefore, I try to discuss the research results on these two types of games as separately as possible.

The game world traditionally distinguishes between six types of video and computer games: (1) platform games, (2) adventures, (3) action games, (4) role-playing games, (5) simulation games, and (6) mental, puzzle, and skill games. Popular games are increasingly being played on the Internet. In most countries, it is possible for children to log onto game sites on which they can play with other visitors. Some sites give the players the possibility of communicating with fellow players during the game.

Platform Games.   Platform games are the most widely played video and computer games. They usually involve a fair bit of action. In platform games the players have to use their skill to get through various levels, and ultimately to the end of the game. Two classic examples of this type of game are Mario, the plumber of Nintendo, and Sonic, the hedgehog of Sega.

Adventures.   These are games in which the player moves through a story, seeing how it develops as he or she goes along. The player controls one of the main characters. This character has to achieve a certain goal, such as solving a murder or finding the Holy Grail. A very popular example of this type of game is Myst.

Action Games.   Action games are sometimes also called Fighters or Shooters. Fighters typically feature a number of different characters, each with different powers, who compete in a martial arts tournament to the death. Examples of fighters include Mortal Kombat, Tekkan, and Streetfighter. Action games often involve a virtual journey through a maze in which the objective is to successfully defeat particular targets, including street fighters, tanks or space monsters. Most games are three-dimensional and are played from the first person perspective. The player looks at the game from the perspective of the main character. So as the player walks along a passage he or she experiences the game environment as the character would see it. Examples of this type of game are Quake and Doom.

Role-Playing Games.   Role-playing games, in short called RPGs, are nearly always set in a fantasy world. The player is assigned a role that has to be kept throughout the course of the game. This may be, for example, a thief or a wizard. If a person plays alone, the other roles are played by the computer. If a person plays with other players, they each have their own roles. In a RPG it is the player who determines what the character does or does not do, and the game develops according to the decisions the players themselves make. An example of this type is the Dungeons and Dragons game.

A certain type of role-playing game that is popular particularly among older adolescents is the Multi-User Dungeon or Domain (MUD). MUDs are virtual environments on the Internet in which users who have logged on can interact with one another. This usually done by text alone. All objects, environments, and characters are described in the text; there are no images whatsoever. These games therefore rely a great deal on the imagination of the players. Each participant plays a fictitious character, who, together with the other characters, creates an interactive story. There are various types of MUDs. Some comprise primarily out of competitive role playing whereby the main objective is to kill monsters. Others, particularly the MOOs (MUD, Object Oriented) are mainly aimed at social communication (Parks & Roberts, 1998).

Simulation Games.   Simulation games try to simulate reality as closely as possible. In the sport and race simulations, the player is a football player or race car driver, in the flying simulations a pilot, and in the battle simulations or strategic war games a soldier. There are also political or economic simulation games in which the player is given a task, for example, building and administrating a city, town, or safari park. An extremely popular simulation game is The Sims in which players simulate characters of different personalities interacting in real-life scenarios. This game is also played online.

Mental, Puzzle, and Skill Games.   This category comprises the traditional board and mental games such as chess, and dominoes but presented as a computer or web game. The most well known and successful in this category is Tetris, which some years ago came standard with a Nintendo game computer. In Tetris the player has to rotate and shift falling blocks in such a way that they form a solid line. There are now many variations of this game. Mental, puzzle, and skill games are played offline as well as online.

In recent years it has often been difficult to place the various games into one of these six categories. The new games in particular are usually a combination of various types of games. A game that contains elements from various types of computer games is called a *hybrid.* This trend of hybridization is seen not only in the video and computer game world. Television programs and films increasingly contain elements that traditionally belong to other genres.

The aim of video and computer games is not always entertainment alone. Much of the educational software, also called *edutainment,* uses elements of the types of games that have been previously described. MUDs also do not always have play and entertainment as the main objective. They can also be used for education, research, and communication.

The Macho World of Video and Computer Games

Many video and computer games present a macho world, where there is little room for women (Dietz, 1998; Kinder, 1991; Provenzo, 1991). In the majority of games, both men and women are portrayed as caricatures. Super heroes in the games are typically tough, exaggeratedly masculine men. Women are often portrayed as a sweet princess or a helpless victim who has to be rescued from the clutches of gorillas or other villains. Many games do not have female characters at all; if they do, the women are typically caricatures: large breasts, curvaceous hips, long legs, dressed in sexy bikinis (Dietz, 1998).

Provenzo (1991) was one of the first to use content analysis to reveal the marginal role of women in the video-game world. Recent content analyses have confirmed this finding. Dietz (1998), who analyzed 33 popular video games, showed that 41% of the video games featured no women at all. In addition, in 28% of the games women were depicted as sex objects and in 21% as victims.

In the past decade, attempts have been made to reverse the traditional roles in video and computer games. By the end of the 1990s some 15% of the video games had a woman as a hero or action figure. These heroines, however, are usually dressed in traditionally feminine clothes. Some women fighters in Mortal Kombat II wear veils, for example (Dietz, 1998).

A famous example of a popular computer game with a female macho hero is the game series Tomb Raider, in which Lara Croft, an archaeologist with very pronounced breasts, has to kill all sorts of bloodthirsty monsters. Initially the question was whether this female protagonist would attract more girls to this type of game. However, this was not the case. The scantily clad Lara Croft primarily won the hearts of boys. For many years she has been the focus of numerous newsgroups and chat rooms used almost exclusively by boys who fantasize about Lara's prominent physical features. In the majority of violent computer games released leading up to the 1990s, women had been portrayed in two extreme ways: as killer or victim. Neither of these roles seemed to appeal to many girls (Subrahmanyam & Greenfield, 1998).

As of the 1990s a relatively large number of video and computer games have been produced that did not feature violence and had a female in the leading role. The computer game industry wanted to make a concerted effort to interest the other half of their target group, and felt that girls could identify better with a female protagonist rather than a male one. This gender-specific marketing of these games was promoted with commercials and packaging featuring a great deal of purple and pink (Subrahmanyam & Greenfield, 1998). As with the violent games, many of these nonviolent games with a female leading character had little success with girls. This is likely explained because in video and computer games there has always been an inextricable link between violence and action. Once the violence had been taken out of the game, the action disappeared as well, and so the games simply became boring (Kinder, 1996; Subrahmanyam & Greenfield, 1998).

However, in the mid-1990s there was a game for girls that suddenly became extremely popular: the computer game Barbie Fashion Designer, which was introduced in 1996. Several million copies of this game were sold worldwide. Although all Barbie games that have since appeared have done fairly well, this one had by far the most impressive sales. The success of this game therefore can not be ascribed just to the lack of violence (Subrahmanyam & Greenfield, 1998). After all, all other Barbie games were based on that same idea. Through this game researchers discovered that it is not so much the lack of violence that attracts girls to playing. It was also shown that girls are not put off by the traditional roles in the video and computer games. Its success was probably due to its combination of realism, femininity of the leading character, and the creative tasks that were set in the game (Subrahmanyam & Greenfield, 1998). In Barbie Fashion Designer girls have to use the computer to design clothes for Barbie. This activity matched the imagination and playing themes of elementary school girls, which reflect their daily experiences more often than those of boys of the same age. Girls of this age tend to prefer realism in their computer games and not the more cartoon-like games that dominate the market, and which boys like so much (Subrahmanyam & Greenfield, 1998).

Violence on the Internet and in Video and Computer Games

The digital media culture of children is full of violence. In the study by Dietz (1998) some 80% of the games she examined contained violence. Practically all these games are based on the principle of the main character having to fight his or her way through various levels. When these games are marketed, a great deal of attention is given to the violence and especially their realism.

> … In Doom you see someone walk through a maze. Suddenly a one-eyed, scary monster comes at you. Then you take your shotgun and shoot it, and you hear 'aaargh.' You see the eye half-hanging out and blood all over the floor. Great fun! (Peter, 13 years old[1])

Even video and computer games that at first sight look innocent contain a great deal of violence. A study carried out by Thompson and Haninger (2001) looked at games that were classified by the American Entertainment Software Rating Board (ESRB) as *Everyone*. Such a classification means that, according to this self-regulatory institute, these games are suitable for all ages. However, the study of Thompson and Haninger revealed that as many as two thirds of these so-called innocent games contain violence. For example, the wounding of human or fantasy characters was rewarded in 69% of these games or was necessary to proceed further.

Within video and computer games there are countless ways for children to come into contact with violence. This is also the case for the Internet. There are undoubtedly fascinating places to visit on the web, but there are also sites where young children should not go. Moreover, the Internet is often inhabited by anonymous people, and it is exactly this anonymity that can, in some people, remove the restraints that prevent certain users from communicating with foul language and lurid suggestions (Kiesler, Siegel, & McGuire, 1984; Walther, Anderson, & Park, 1994).

---

[1]Taken from Ankersmit and Van Veen (1995).

Conclusion.   I have outlined a number of distinctive characteristics of the digital media culture of children. I have shown that there is an increasing convergence of both the content and the technologies used. Not only are the traditional boundaries between entertainment and advertising disappearing, but there is also an integration of their applications: Computer games are becoming Web games; and while playing Web games, children can listen to digital music and get into contact with individuals from all over the world, for example via Instant Messaging.

I have also pointed at the growing commercialization of the digital children's culture. The most popular children's sites are not those of public institutes, but commercial companies who use these sites primarily to offer children entertainment in branded communities (Montgommery, 2000). If this trend continues, the social and cultural needs of children of today and of future generations will be primarily defined in relation to commercial media products and manufacturers (Buckingham, 2000).

Another characteristic of the digital children's culture is the fragmentation of audiences. Because media manufacturers are able to determine narrowly defined user profiles, they are becoming increasingly better at niche marketing, whereby commercial entertainment is being offered that closely fits in with the preferences of small, distinct target groups (see Turow, 2001). The children's media market, in contrast to the past, is lucrative, with today's children having not only their own television channels, but also their own Web games, IM software, and Web sites. It is beyond doubt that these developments present extra challenges to parents, educators, and legislators (Turow, 2001).

ACCESS TO INTERACTIVE MEDIA

How frequently do children use the Internet? What do boys and girls do when they are online? What does the ideal children's Web site look like? Which children play games? What is so fascinating about video and computer games? The answers to these questions are addressed in this section. First, I look at the use of the Internet, after which I will review children's use of video and computer games.

Access to the Internet

Over the past 5 years, the number of Internet users worldwide has grown from 25 to 500 million. If we compare this to other media, the spread of the Internet has taken place at an unprecedented rate. The telephone reached the milestone of 500 million only after 45 years, and even television took 15 years to do so. The use of the Internet among children over the past few years has increased to such an extent that all study results are outdated before they are actually published. However, I would still like to start with a few figures. At present, more than three fourths of children between 7 and 13 are online, either through access from home or through school. This applies to American children as well as Dutch and British children (U.S. Census Bureau, 2001; NOP Research Group, 2001; Valkenburg & Buijzen, 2003).

Once children are online they may remain there on average between 30 minutes to an hour. Preadolescents (10 to 13 years of age) use the Internet more frequently than younger children (7 to 9 years of age), and are also online for longer. Girls and boys do not significantly differ in the frequency with which they use the Internet, and they stay online for more or less the same duration (Valkenburg & Buijzen, 2003).

Why do Children Use the Internet?

Do children use the Internet primarily for entertainment, or do they use it mainly for information, communication, or social purposes? We investigated these questions through a survey study among 194 children between 8 and 13 years with home access to the Internet. Our study showed that children use the Internet for a variety of reasons. The primary reason has to do with an affinity with the computer. Children like working with the computer and are curious to see what the Internet has to offer them. Another important reason for using the Internet was to find information on their hobbies and idols and for carrying out school assignments (Valkenburg & Soeters, 2001).

Social interaction (e.g., making new friends; getting to know other children) was also important, especially for the 10- to 13-year-olds. At about 10 years of age, children's need for online social interaction with peers usually rapidly increases. In this period, children's friendships usually proliferate and their concern with interpersonal identity becomes more important (Valkenburg & Soeters, 2001).

What do Children Like About the Internet?

In our survey study, we asked children to give a spontaneous description of something they had enjoyed on the Internet. Playing computer games was the most frequently mentioned, by girls (18%) and boys (16%) alike. Watching and listening to video clips was also mentioned often, by 17% of the girls and 10% of the boys. Children often said they enjoyed visiting their favorite children's Web site, again equally among girls and boys (13% and 12%, respectively).

The spontaneous descriptions of children did yield some important differences among girls and boys. First, only boys (7%) mentioned the downloading of *codes* and *cheats* as something they enjoyed doing. Codes or cheats are pieces of software to improve the conditions of a computer game, for example by obtaining more lives or energy. Codes and cheats are often used in certain types of computer games that are particularly popular among boys, such as shooters or fighters. In addition, only boys spontaneously mentioned enjoying visiting sensational Internet sites (violence and pornography). Boys of this age generally have a higher need for sensation than girls have (Zuckerman, 1979) and their choice for sensational sites may reflect this need. Other differences in the descriptions given included that it was girls who enjoyed searching for information on the Web, for example about their idols or animals. Girls also enjoyed more than boys chatting and meeting other people on the Web. In summary, our surveys suggest that girls and boys did not differ so much in the time they spend on the Internet and in their general motives for using the Internet, but rather they differ considerably in what they enjoy doing on the Internet.

What is the Ideal Children's Entertainment Site?

In another survey study among 399 7- to 13-year-olds, we asked children to indicate what their ideal entertainment Web site would be (Valkenburg & Buijzen, 2003).This question was investigated by presenting children with a list of known activities of children's Web sites and asking them how important it was that the activities were featured on a Web site. Table 6.2 lists the various Web site activities with the most popular on top and the least popular on the bottom.

Playing games was the most preferred activity offered by a children's Web site. This finding held for both younger and older children, and for boys and girls. Other important Web site activities included the ability to find information, listen to music, and download games and film clips.

Children's preferences for web activities differed significantly for older and younger children, especially in the case of communication technologies. Ten- to thirteen-year-old children showed a significantly stronger preference for communication technologies, such as chatting, e-mailing, and using SMS via the Web site, than the 7- to 9-year-olds did. This age difference is in line with theories on children's emotional and social development. From about ten years of age, children are increasingly interested in developing social relationships. At this time, their need for intimacy emerges (Sullivan, 1953), and their concern with interpersonal identity becomes far more acute (e.g., Allison & Schulz, 2001).

Children's favorite web activities also differed significantly between boys and girls. Boys more often preferred to download games and video clips, whereas girls more often preferred to e-mail and to send digital cards on the

TABLE 6.2

"On My Favorite Web Site I Would Like to ..."

	Boys (% yes)	Girls (% yes)	7- to 9-year-olds (% yes)	10- to 13-year-olds (% yes)
... play games	84	87	84	85
... find information	81	79	84	78
... listen to music	72	73	71	74
... download games	82[b]	59[a]	63[x]	77[y]
... download clips	72[b]	55[a]	58	68
... be able to chat	56[a]	71[b]	51[x]	71[y]
... be able to email	52[a]	64[b]	52	60
... send digital postcards	46[a]	61[b]	54	52
... be able to use SMS	38	41	28	46

Note. Adopted from Valkenburg & Buijzen (2003).
[a,b; x,y] Differences between boys versus girls and younger versus older children were significant at $p < 0.05$.

Internet. Finally, girls had a clearer preference for chat and Instant Messaging. This gender-specific preference for communication technologies of the Internet is not surprising. If one investigates the history of communication technologies, it has usually been females who first embraced such technologies. This trend was shown when the telephone was introduced (Rakow, 1988), and one century later, the mobile telephone seems to be following the same pattern. Market research has shown that it is again women, and particularly teenage girls, who are the trendsetters of mobile phone use. In the past few years, Instant Messaging can be added to the list of technologies that satisfy preadolescent girls' relatively high need for communication and social interaction (see also Lenhart, Rainee, & Lewis, 2001).

Access to Video and Computer Games

As discussed earlier, many studies into the use of electronic games have made no distinction between video and computer games. This makes it difficult to draw any reliable conclusions regarding the use of these games, as these types of games are used differently by various demographic subgroups. In contrast to most other media, video games are played relatively more by children from families with a lower socioeconomic status, whereas this tends to be the opposite for computer games (Roberts et al., 1999). Video games are also mostly played by 8- to 13-year olds, whereas computer games are played more by very young children and adolescents (Roberts et al., 1999; Woodard & Gridina, 2000).

A series of studies, particularly those conducted in the 1980s, have shown that boys spend about three times as much time playing video games than girls do (e.g., Dominick, 1984; Kubey & Larson, 1990; Lin & Lepper, 1987). Market data from game manufacturers in the 1980s also showed that approximately three fourths of the video games that were released were bought by boys. However, it is important to note here that these early studies concerned video games, as very few computer games were available at that time.

The large differences in video game use between boys and girls was regarded as a serious problem in the 1980s. Video games were seen as a stepping stone to the adult digital world where a proficiency at working with computers is essential. It was feared that the gap between boys and girls would increase, with the danger of girls being left at a disadvantage in later life (e.g., Greenfield, 1984; Kinder, 1991).

However, in the past decades the initial worries about girls' moderate use of video games have increasingly been abandoned by researchers. Although boys still tend to play video games three to five times as much as girls, the total time that boys and girls spend on a computer does not differ much: Both boys and girls spend an average of three fourths of an hour per day on the computer (Robert et al., 1999). It also appears that with computer games the differences between boys and girls are far less than with video games. Until the age of 7, girls and boys spend the same amount of time on computer games. In the age group 8 to 13, boys play somewhat more, but this is only a matter of a few minutes per day (19 vs. 11 min.). Only among adolescents is there a significant difference between boys and girls: Boys from the ages of 14 to 18 spend an average of 16 minutes per day on computer games and girls only 5 minutes (Roberts et al., 1999).

The decrease in the differences between the sexes in the use of interactive media since the second half of the 1990s may have something to do with the fact that the computer game culture is less violent and macho than the video game culture. Although there are many violent computer games on the market, there is a far greater variety of computer games than video games. Educational games, for example, are almost exclusively computer games. In the study of Roberts et al. (1999), children who had played a video or computer game the previous day were asked what sort of game it was. Of those who had played a video game, 42% of the children had played an action game, whereas this was the case for only 19% for those who had played a computer game. Moreover, in the case of computer games 28% of the children mentioned playing an educational game, whereas there were no children who had played an educational video game.

The decreasing differences between the genders in the use of computer games is also seen in our Internet study, which showed that girls enjoy playing web games as much as boys do. Girls gave the same importance as boys to the ability to play web games on a Web site. However, boys and girls differ in the type of games they prefer to play. This was shown, for example, in our findings that only boys, and no girls, liked to download codes and cheats. Because codes and cheats are used relatively frequently when playing violent action games, this result suggest that boys and girls prefer to play different computer games (Valkenburg & Soeters, 2001).

In summary, although the initial worries about unequal access for boys and girls to interactive media were perhaps well-founded, there is now less reason to be anxious about a possible disadvantageous position for girls. The insights offered above also suggest that future academic studies should make a clear distinction between the uses and effects of video versus computer games.

The Appeal of Video and Computer Games

Children tend to use the computer and the Internet primarily to play games. Video and computer games seem to have a universal appeal to children. This is primarily due to the content and quality of the games. Manufacturers of games take good account of the preferences of their target group and closely follow new trends in youth culture (Kinder, 1991). The latest generation of computer games provides action, speed, appealing music, good sound effects, and graphics of film quality. However, computer games have also a number of other features that keep children glued to the screen.

Challenges at the Right Level. Good quality games are created in such a way that they provide the player with a constant challenge that is just within his or her capabilities. Most games are relatively easy at the start and then become increasingly difficult throughout the course of the game. In this way at every level, the player faces a new challenge that is just within his or her grasp, and the greater the challenge that has been overcome, the greater the satisfaction. The pleasure derived from overcoming such obstacles can be explained by Zillmann's (1978) theory of excitation transfer, which was discussed in chapter 4. Trying to overcome obstacles is an activity that increases the level of arousal in children. Once the obstacle has been overcome the child experiences relief, but because the level of arousal is still high in the child, the feeling of relief is even more intense. In other words, children who have just experienced some tension, feel extra relief and satisfaction once the obstacle has been conquered. This might explain why overcoming obstacles in computer games is so enjoyable.

Possibilities for Active Control. In contrast to watching television, video and computer games offer the possibility of active control. Most games give room for free choice. The player can choose for himself or herself elements such as color, background, level of difficulty, character, blood, or no blood. In some games the progress of the game can even be determined by the player himself. According to Fritz (1995) it is those children who are struggling with their own physical and emotional development who like to have some control over their game. Video and computer games give them the opportunity to have everything temporarily under control, and that gives a pleasant feeling.

Immediate Feedback and Reward. When watching a film an observer can only experience the successes and experiences of others through empathy. In video and computer games, however, the player can experience the successes and rewards himself or herself. As with playing sports and music the player receives immediate feedback. If the preceding action has been successful, the player is rewarded immediately. This ongoing reward structure is a strong stimulus to carry on playing.

Stimulating Curiosity. Video and computer games play very much on the curiosity of the players. Just as in a book or television series with an exciting story, users want to know how the story will end. Also during the game, things are constantly happening that stimulate the player's curiosity. Players can, for example, come across a secret cassette tape or a closed box or door that they have to open. This is different from films, in which the curiosity is stimulated by temporarily keeping information from the viewer. Computer games stimulate the curiosity more than traditional media do because an answer to this sort of conundrum is often necessary before the player can continue (Grodal, 2000).

Possibility for Identification. Video and computer games have all the necessary characteristics that are known to lead to intense involvement and identification. They have super heroes of all shapes and sizes, who operate in a fantasy world full of mysterious powers and bizarre adventures. Moreover, all this happens in an atmosphere and with music that closely fits in with the latest trends in youth culture. Many games make use of the *first-person perspective*, whereby, as mentioned before, the player experiences the game environment from the perspective of the hero. This helps to increase identification with the protagonists. The player actually becomes the hero:

> I actually feel that I am in the game itself ... sometimes during Doom I'm so frightened ... my heart goes boom, boom, boom ... that I just want to stop playing. In Doom there was this room ... you had to play in the dark, the only thing you could see was the machine gun fire coming from the other gun, only then

could you shoot back, and then you heard a scream if you hit him. I thought: I'm not playing this anymore, and so I got a code to switch on the lights. (Mattew, 14 years old[2])

Possibility of Playing Together.   Many games provide the possibility to play with others, either online or offline. A study carried out by Van Schie, Wiegman, Kuttschreuter, and Boer (1996) revealed that 68% of children usually played video or computer games with other children. Playing games on the web can be very exciting for children. Game sites usually allow you to play against friends or unknown players. It is not known how often children use these interactive game sites. However, what we do know is that both girls and boys often enjoy playing web games of all sorts on the Internet (Valkenburg & Buijzen, 2003).

EFFECTS OF INTERACTIVE MEDIA

Research into the effects of interactive media is very much in its infancy. Most of the research until now has focused on video games, with only a few studies looking at the Internet. The views on the effect of interactive media on children differ greatly. Proponents usually mention the positive effects, such as improving eye–hand coordination, spatial intelligence, and the possibility of playing together (e.g., Griffith, Voloschin, Gibb, & Bailey, 1983). Opponents claim that interactive media take too much time away from other activities, such as homework, reading, and sports. They also believe that interactive media make children lonely and impoverish their social contacts or even impair their creativity, as players often do no more than closely follow preset rules (see Subrahmanyam, Greenfield, Kraut, & Gross, 2001). There are also opponents who believe that violent computer games make children aggressive (e.g., Anderson & Dill, 2000). In this section, I draw on academic research to highlight a number of positive and negative effects of interactive media. These effects have been grouped into physical, cognitive, and social effects.

Physical Effects

Can children get epileptic seizures from using interactive media? Is there a risk of Repetitive Strain Injury (RSI) among children who use computers? The research literature on the physical effects of computer games on children have so far focused only on the effects of video games on epileptic seizures during or after playing, and on the effects of playing video games on RSI, or an RSI-related complaint: *Nintendonitis.*

---

[2]Taken from Ankersmit and Van Veen (1995).

Epileptic Seizures.   Particularly in the 1980s, several reports appeared in the media regarding children who had suffered epileptic seizures is a result of playing video games. This phenomenon also received some attention in the academic literature. These epileptic seizures are primarily caused by a specific form of epilepsy, photosensitive epilepsy, when the child is over-sensitive to flickering lights. The symptoms vary from headaches and changes in the field of vision to nervous tics, dizziness, confusion, reduced awareness, and seizures. The symptoms disappear as soon as the child stops playing. The chance that the child will be affected is reduced the further the child sits from the screen and the better the quality of the screen: 100Hz screens seem to be better than 50Hz screens (Badinand-Hubert et al., 1998; Graf, Chatrian, Glass, & Knauss, 1994).

RSI and "Nintendonitis."   Children often sit in front of the screen focused and tense. If they sit too long in this posture, they run the risk, as do adults, of developing RSI: pain in the elbow and wrist or a lack of feeling in the lower or upper arm. With the increasing use of computers among children, RSI is a growing problem. A special form of RSI seen among some children is a phenomenon that has been called *Nintendonitis.* This is a play on words with the medical term *tendinitis,* an inflammation of the tendon, and the Nintendo console. Nintendonitis results from making quick movements for a long period of time with the thumb on the controller of game computers (Macgregor, 2000).

Cognitive Effects

Cognitive effects relate to knowledge and understanding. A number of studies have been conducted into the cognitive effects of using computers at school. These studies found, for example, that children's knowledge of biology or meteorology increased because of using certain computer applications (see Roschelle, Pea, Hoadley, Gordin, & Means, 2000). In this chapter, I do not go into detail into these school-related studies. Rather, I deal with the effects of interactive media in children's everyday home environment. These latter types of studies are aimed at the incidental learning effects of interactive media. I will discuss research carried out into the following four cognitive effects: intelligence, eye–hand coordination, visual attentional capacity, and creativity.

Intelligence.   Some researchers believe that children become more intelligent through using computers and playing electronic games. This hypothesis is in part based on the so called *Flynn effect* (Flynn, 1999). As discussed in chapter 1, Flynn compared the scores of the intelligence tests in 14 countries, including the United States, Germany, France, and the Netherlands. In almost all countries, he observed a significant increase in IQ in the past decades. The increases in IQ of young people is seen particularly in nonverbal tests, in which figurative factors play an important role (Flynn, 1999). Because the assignments in this figural intelligence test are similar to certain tasks in computer games, some researchers assume that it is the electronic games that have increased the intelligence scores in the past decades (Greenfield, 1998; Neisser, 1998).

To confirm the hypothesis that the computer helps to make children more intelligent it has to be shown that the differences in intelligence that have been found between different generations of children also apply to children within generations. In other words, if computers and computer games are indeed responsible for the difference in intelligence between generations, then children from the same generation should differ in intelligence according to how much they use the computer. Although there are a few studies that have found small to moderate effects on the learning process, until now no research has proven that today's children who use the computer frequently are more intelligent than those who do not.

However, there are some indications that a certain form of intelligence, namely spatial intelligence, can be stimulated by playing computer games. Spatial intelligence has to do with remembering the shape of objects and understanding how these objects fit in or alongside other objects. A test for spatial intelligence has been included in practically all the standard intelligence tests. Some studies suggest that children who regularly play computer games develop a better spatial intelligence. For example, in a study by Okagaki and Frensch (1994) a group of teenagers played the puzzle game Tetris for 6 hours. None of these teenagers was familiar with the game. After 6 hours of playing Tetris the spatial intelligence of both girls and boys was seen to improve. It is not only puzzle games that can improve spatial intelligence; other games have this potential as well (Greenfield, Brannon, & Lohr, 1994; Subrahmanyam & Greenfield, 1994).

Eye–Hand Coordination.   Eye–hand coordination is the skill of responding immediately with the hands to what the eye has just seen. Eye–hand coordination is important in, for example, typing, as well as in operating machines, driving cars, trains, and flying airplanes. For dentists, watchmakers, and all other professions that require a high degree of dexterity, good eye–hand coordination is essential. Some types of computer games, especially the platform and action games, require a high level of eye–hand coordination. Many researchers consequently believe that playing these sorts of games stimulates the eye–hand coordination (e.g., Griffith et al., 1983).

However, not much research has been carried out into whether electronic games actually stimulate eye–hand coordination. A study carried out by Gagnon (1985) did not find any effects. However, this study measured the eye–hand coordination using a paper test in which the children using a pencil had to quickly draw a dot in a series of circles. It is possible that this form of measurement was too far removed from the eye–hand coordination required by electronic games to make a comparison. After all, electronic games primarily involve following moving objects. Three other studies, which used tests that fell within the aforementioned definition of eye–hand coordination, did find a positive effect (Greenfield, de Winstanley, Kilpatric, & Kaye, 1994; Griffith et al., 1983; Kuhlman & Beitel, 1991).

Visual Attentional Capacity.   Playing video games not only seems to stimulate eye-hand coordination and spatial attention, but there are also indications that they may increase a player's visual attentional capacity. In a study by Green and Bavelier (2003), the attentional capacity of video-game players (VGPs) was compared to that of non-video-game players (NVGPs). A VGP was defined as a person that had played video games on at least 4 days per week for a minimum of 1 hour per day for the previous 6 months. The video games included Grand Theft Auto3, Half-life, Counter Strike, Crazy Taxi, and Super Mario Cart (Green & Bavelier, 2003).

Green and Bavelier's study consisted of four quasiexperiments, in which a different measure of attentional capacity was used. In one experiment, for example, subjects were asked to decide as quickly as possible whether a square or a diamond appeared within one of six rings that were presented on a screen, while ignoring a series of distractor shapes that appeared outside the rings. In all experiments, it was found that VGPs were significantly better or faster able to monitor objects in their visual field than did NVGPs.

However, as discussed in chapter 3, in quasiexperiments subjects are not randomly assigned to either the experimental or treatment condition. In Green and Bavelier's (2003) study, the attentional capacities of existing groups of VGPs and NVGPs were compared. Therefore, these researchers could not rule out the possibility that differences in attentional capacity between VGPs and NVGPs were due to initial differences between the players, rather than to true experimental effects. To rule out this possible validity threat, Green and Bavelier conducted an additional experiment that only used NVGPs. In this training experiment, one group of NVGPs were asked to play the action video game Medal of Honor for 1 hour per day for 10 consecutive days. A second group, which served as a control group, was asked to play the puzzle video game Tetris, which would not be expected to change a player's attentional capacity. After 10 days, only the action players (and not the Tetris players) showed a significant increase in their test performances (Green & Bavelier, 2003).

Creativity.   There are some people who are convinced that computer games make children less creative, as the games have to be played according to rules that have been determined beforehand, so that nothing is left to the player to discover for himself or herself. Although there is no empirical evidence to confirm or refute this claim, there are several a priori arguments that should be considered. It is indeed not good for the creative development of children to be confronted solely with games that are fixed by set rules, such as ludo and goose (see Valkenburg, 2001). However, it is incorrect to suggest that all video and computer games are played according to predetermined rules. In some games, children are able to give their imaginations free rein. They can, for example, make drawings, compose music, and write creative stories.

There are as of yet no studies that show that computer games can make children more creative. However, one study has shown that children who worked for 6 months with the computer program, Logo, in the classroom were more creative than children who had not played with this game (Clements, 1991). Developed by Seymour Papert, Logo is a computer program whereby children, through instructions given to a tortoise, can draw lines and figures on the computer. Although there has not yet been any research that shows that computer games can make children more creative, it is quite conceivable that certain adventures, RPG's and simulation games designed to stimulate the creativity of children do actually have this effect (see Valkenburg, 2001).

Emotional and Social Effects

Do children become lonely if they spend too much time on the Internet? Do interactive media undermine family relationships? Do children sometimes get scared of what they find on the Internet? Do children become aggressive from playing violent computer games? In this last section, I outline the latest research into the emotional and social effects of interactive media. I start by discussing the displacement hypothesis, after which I look at the effects of interactive media on family relationships and friendships, fear and uneasiness, and aggression.

Displacement Effects.   Many parents and teachers are worried that the time children spend on interactive media will be at the expense of other activities that are beneficial for their development, such as homework, sports, music, and interacting with children of their own age. Not much research has been carried out into displacement effects of computers. The available research primarily looks at the extent to which the increased use of computers has reduced the time spent watching television (see Subrahmanyam et al., 2001).

As explained earlier, computer games have a number of specific characteristics that keep children glued to their screens. A study carried out by Egli and Meyers (1984) revealed that children who had just got a new computer game would rather do nothing else for several weeks than play their new game. But with the majority of children after these initial weeks the novelty had worn off a fair bit, with their playing frequency returning back to the level of before the new game. A small group of children, however, remained under the spell of the computer game for quite some time, becoming restless if they were not able to play and sacrificing other social activities in order to be able to carry on with their game. A survey carried out by Griffiths and Hunt (1995) shows that 7% of 12- to 16-year olds spend more than 4.5 hours per day playing computer games. It is clear that with these children, playing computer games would certainly be at the expense of other important activities (Griffiths, 1998).[3]

Family Relations. An important concern about the Internet is that it encourages children to spend more time alone in front of the screen, talking to strangers, and forming online friendships instead of friendships with their real-life peers. Because these online friendships are seen as superficial, "easy in, easy out" relationships that lack a common set of values and feelings of affection and obligation, it is believed that the Internet increases social isolation and fragmentation of families and social groups (Locke, 1998; Putnam, 2000).

Evidence to support this media-induced fragmentation hypothesis is mixed. An early study carried out when the game console first came onto the market showed that the game computer had a positive effect on family relationships. At the time, the game computer brought parents and children together to play video games and discover new things (Mitchel, 1985). This integrating function was also seen when television was introduced. When televisions first appeared in the 1950s, it was believed that they had an integrating function within the family. The television was initially considered a sort of cinema, and family and neighbors would come together and socialize. However, in the course of time this function of the television has completely disappeared, for a variety of reasons. Not only have the number of channels and programs increased considerably over the past few decades but also most families have two or more televisions in the home. The remote control may also have played a role in the division of the family as a common target group. In many families the remote control is operated usually by one, sometimes two, family members (usually men), who discourage family viewing by driving off other family members (Walker & Bellamy, 2001).

It is a question whether the computer still has a positive effect on family communication and cohesion, now that most children have a computer or game computer in their own room, and many children's technological knowl-

---

[3]Mark Griffiths (1998) stated in his article that 20% of the children can be classified as dependent upon computer games. I believe that this figure is too high. Griffiths suggested that children who scored higher than 4 on a scale ranging from 1 to 8 are dependent upon computer games. However, the first four questions of the scale are so general that practically all players could give a positive answer to them. For example: Do you often play every day?, Do you often play for long periods of time?, Do you play for the excitement or the kick?, And do you play to improve your score? It seems to me unfair to label children who answer these questions positively as *dependent upon (addicted to) computer games.*

edge is far greater than that of their parents (Lenhart et al., 2001; Valkenburg, 2002). There are not many indications to show that the modern computer and game console help to bring families together. A study carried out by Roberts (2000) showed that 61% of 12- to 17-year-olds use the Internet usually alone and that 64% of them normally played computer games on their own. A study by Turow and Nir (2000) conducted among children has revealed that 50% of parents believed that family members who spend a great deal of time online talk with the family less than they would do otherwise.

Finally, a study by Kraut et al. (1998) demonstrated that the use of the Internet went together with a small, although significant, reduction in family communication. In this 5-year longitudinal research project, 93 American families were followed during two time spans: from 1995 to 1997 (Kraut et al., 1998), and from 1998 to 1999 (Kraut et al., 2002). The initial study demonstrated that using the Internet for as little as 30 minutes per day led to small, although significant declines in family communication. However, in the follow-up study, these aversive Internet effects disappeared: Time spent on the Internet tended to be positively related to family communication. The discrepancy between the results of the initial and those of the follow-up study by Kraut et al. suggests that the Internet initially can replace a small portion of time spent with family members, but that this displacement effect dissipates as soon as family members have gained experience with the technology.

Friendships and Loneliness.   Children regularly use the Internet for communication and social interaction with friends and potential friends. However, there are as yet few indications to show that the Internet facilitates primarily superficial contacts. A survey by Wolak, Mitchell, and Finkelhor (2002) carried out among 1,500 American children revealed that 17% of children between the ages of 10 and 17 had at some time in the last year developed a close friendship with a person they had met online. A close friend was defined as someone with whom you could speak about things that were important to you. In a survey by Lenhart et al. (2001) conducted among 754 12- to 17-year-olds, 48% of the respondents said that the Internet had actually improved their relationships with their friends, and 32% said that the Internet helped them in making new friends. The majority (61%) of the respondents felt that the Internet did not take away time that they would otherwise spend with their friends. However, a small group (10%) did feel that the Internet made them spend less time with their friends, although they did feel that they were better able to keep in contact with friends who lived far away.

A special case in communication via the Internet involves the MUDs. In MUDs it is common practice to experiment with your identity. Children can therefore pretend to be an older person, someone from the opposite sex, or even someone without any particular sex. What do MUD visitors think of online friendships? This was investigated in a study by Parks and Roberts (1998) among 235 MUD participants, who primarily consisted of adolescents. Nearly all participants had developed at least one personal relationship when participating in the MUD games. The majority had made between 4 and 15 contacts. Various types of relationships had developed, but most contacts were described by the respondents as close friendships (41%), friendships (26%) and romantic relationships (26%). There were significant differences in the time spent on the various friendships. Romantic relationships received more time, followed by close friendships and then friendships.

In summary, several surveys have shown that children and adolescents regularly form online contacts and friendships. However, such observations do not allow for the inference that the Internet stimulates the social involvement of children and adolescents. To draw such a conclusion, one needs to know more about the quality of children's online relationships, and about the impact of the Internet on children's offline social relationships. The study by Kraut et al. (1998) demonstrated that Internet use led to increases in adolescents' loneliness, and decreases in their offline social involvement, although their follow-up study could again not replicate their initial results (Kraut et al., 2002). In this second study, the authors even found a small positive relationship between hours spent on the Internet and the number of contacts with whom adolescents kept up.

The studies conducted so far give little cause to suggest that the Internet isolates children from their peers and social contacts. However, there is still little known about the social effects of excessive Internet use. As is the case with other media, it is plausible that there would be a small group of Internet users who spend so much time online that all sorts of offline activities are pushed to the side. No research has been carried out into the implications of this sort of excessive Internet use among children and adolescents.

Fear and Uneasiness.   Another concern about the Internet is that children are exposed to inappropriate or violent material, which can make them feel uneasy or upset them. On the Internet children run three risks. First, as is the case with traditional media such as television and film, they can come across violence and pornography, which may upset them. The Internet, however, has two additional risks. Children can be harassed when online, in chat rooms or via e-mail and IM messages, but they can also be harassed offline if they have given out their address or arranged a personal meeting.

This first risk of the Internet occurs regularly. In a survey conducted by Mitchel, Finkelhor, and Wolak (2001) among children of 10 to 17 years of age, one fourth of the respondents admitted to unintentionally coming across sexual material. This occurred during surfing (via searches, incorrectly spelled addresses, and by clicking links by accident or otherwise) or by opening spam mail and clicking on their links. Twenty-three percent of the children who came across this material were either very or extremely upset or embarrassed by viewing this material.

The second risk, online harassment (insults, threats of physical violence), was experienced by 6% of the children during the last year. These threats occurred mainly in chat rooms (33%), via IM (32%), and e-mail (19%). In two thirds of the cases (62%), these threats came from strangers. Thirty-three percent of the children who were harassed had become very or extremely frightened by the threats. The threats were experienced more by older than younger children.

No child experienced offline harassment. However, 16% of the children had at some time a close online friendship, of which 3% were with an adult. This occurred mainly through chat rooms or MUDs. In the majority of cases (69%), these friendships also resulted in contacts outside the web, through the telephone or ordinary mail. On occasion, there were actually meetings between children and adults. One girl of 16 said that via the Internet she had met up with a man of between 30 and 40. The meeting took place in a public place, where he said he wanted to go to bed with her. She refused.

One of our surveys conducted among children between 8 and 13 years of age also revealed that a small group of children had experienced online harassment, although offline harassment hardly or never occurred (Valkenburg & Soeters, 2001). The results of Mitchel et al.'s (2001) survey certainly demonstrate that children regularly have offline contact with fellow Internet users. Offline harassment is therefore a potential risk of the Internet, which has to be taken very seriously.

Aggression.   In the past two decades, numerous studies have been carried out into the influence of video games such as Mortal Kombat and Dactyl Nightmare on the aggressive behavior of children. At the start of the millennium, two meta-analyses on this subject were published almost at the same time. As defined in chapter 3, meta-analyses are studies in which the results of all previous studies are reanalyzed and re-evaluated. Both meta-analyses on the effect of video and computer games reported a correlation between violent games and aggressive behavior that is classified in the literature as small to moderate. Sherry (2001) found a correlation of $r = 0.15$, and Anderson and Bushman (2001) found a slightly higher correlation of $r = 0.19$.

If we compare the results of these meta-analyses with the meta-analysis of Paik and Comstock (1994) on the effect of film and television violence, then we would have to conclude that the effect of video and computer games on aggression is lower than that of film and television violence because in the meta-analysis of Paik and Comstock (1994) a correlation of $r = 0.31$ was found. This difference in effect size may have to do with the fact that in earlier video games the violence was not very realistic, so that it is taken less seriously by children than television and film violence. Anderson and Bushman (2001) as well as Sherry (2001) included a large number of empirical studies from the 1980s in their meta-analyses. At that time the quality of the video games could not really be compared to that of television violence, as clearly indicated by the following review of the video games Mortal Kombat and Night Trap, published in the early 1990s:

> The figures move woodenly on the Mortal Kombat screen .... The image produced by the game is ten times as unclear as what you would normally see on television. What's more, the pictures of Night Trap are so faint that they look more like a badly constructed mosaic than a film picture.

Sherry (2001) found that recent video and computer games had a greater effect on aggressive behavior than video and computer games produced in the 1980s. This finding offers an explanation of why Anderson and Bushman (2001) found a greater effect in their meta-analysis than Sherry. In fact, Anderson and Bushman included a greater percentage of recent studies in their meta-analysis. More specifically, the meta-analysis by Anderson and Bushman consisted of 44% studies carried out in the 1980s, whereas that of Sherry comprised of 60% studies conducted in the 1980s. It is therefore quite likely that future meta-analyses on the effect of video and computer games will show correlations that are similar to those found for the effect of film and television violence.

Although both meta-analyses clearly show that video and computer games can promote aggressive behavior, it is of course equally important to know how this happens. As the graphics of the latest generation of video and computer games are very similar to those in films, some explanations of the influence of film and TV violence can certainly be used to analyze the effects of violent games.

Social Learning.   The social learning theory of Bandura (1986) states that children learn aggressive behavior from television by observing the aggressive behavior of their TV heroes and in particular the consequences of this behavior. This learning of aggression occurs particularly when the child identifies with the TV hero and when the aggressive behavior of the TV hero is rewarded. Video and computer games provide players with ample possibilities for identification (Kinder, 1991). In many games, the player even plays the role of the main character, which further stimulates the possibilities for identification.

The reward aspect of Bandura (1986) also plays an important role in video and computer games. After all, in many video and computer games each well executed violent action is rewarded immediately. This can be in the form of extra lives, power, energy, or ammunition or through direct compliments, such as in Mortal Kombat: "You are the supreme warrior!" Violent video games teach players the same lesson as violent films and TV series: Violence is an effective means to solve a conflict.

Arousing Violence.   The second explanation for the influence of TV violence, as illustrated in chapter 3, is that exciting violent programs make children so restless that afterward they become more aggressive in their play and interaction with other children. This explanation can be applied to video and computer games as well because these games also bring about intense physical arousal among children. In the meta-analysis of Anderson and Bushman (2001) a significant positive correlation of $r = 0.22$ was found between playing games and physical arousal. In violent games the violence is usually combined with plenty of action, speed, and rousing music. It is therefore very likely that children, after playing these kinds of games—just as after watching violence in films and television—remain restless and as a result show aggressive behavior in their play and interaction with other children.

Cognitive Script, Priming, and Desensitization Theories.   The explanations of the cognitive script, priming, and desensitization theories can also be applied to the effect of violent games (see chap. 3, this volume). If film and television violence is able to teach children aggressive scripts and prime aggressive thoughts, then video and computer games could probably do the same. In addition, it is conceivable that desensitization occurs with video and computer games, particularly because the violence in the latest generation of games has a realism and detail that is very similar to that of film and television violence.

Aggression Through Frustration.   One of the most important differences between television and video and computer games is that a gamer can either win or lose, whereas a television viewer can not. Because many video and computer games provide a constant challenge by becoming increasingly difficult, fights end more often than not in failure. It is therefore possible that the player becomes frustrated when playing the game. According to Dollard et al. (1939), frustration can lead to aggression if someone fails to reach his or her goal time and again. The frustration–aggression assumption was investigated in a Dutch study by Marcel Keij (1995), in which a number of boys from 12 to 18 years of age played the video game Mortal Kombat. None of them had played the game before. For one group of boys, before play started, Keij introduced a special simplification code to the game, which increased the chance of winning a fight (the winning group). With a second group of boys, just before the end of the game, Keij secretly pressed the reset button of the computer causing the game to suddenly stop (the bad-luck group). With the other boys (the third group) he did nothing. Because these boys were playing the game for the first time, it was likely that they would lose the fight (the losing group). To make the frustration on losing as great as possible, the participants were told that previous players had achieved very good results with the game and that the best players would get a CD voucher. The boys from the bad-luck group, who were probably the most frustrated of all, at the end were almost twice as aggressive as the boys from the winning group. The boys from the losing group had aggression levels somewhere between the other two groups. This study suggests that frustration in combination with violence in video and computer games is a possible cause for the increase in aggressive behavior after a fight game.

Conclusion.   Video and computer games have various positive and negative effects on the development of children. Children who spend a great deal of time playing these games may develop better eye–hand coordination, spatial awareness as well as visual attentional capacity (Green & Bavelier, 2003; Griffith et al., 1983; Okagaki & Frensch, 1994). However, it is not wise to spend too much time on these games, as complaints such as RSI and Nintendonitis may result, and above all, playing may come at the expense of other activities such as homework, reading, social contacts and sports. The negative effects of video and computer games are primarily influenced by the content of the games. A series of empirical studies and two meta-analyses have shown that the violence in the games can stimulate aggressive thoughts and behavior (see Anderson & Bushman, 2001; Anderson & Dill, 2000; Sherry, 2001).

References

Acuff, D. S. (1997). *What kids buy and why: The psychology of marketing to kids.* New York: Free Press.

Adams, R. J. (1987). An evaluation of color preference in early infancy. *Infant Behavior and Development, 10*, 143–150.

Allison, B., & Schultz, J. B. (2001). Interpersonal identity formation during early adolescence. *Adolescence, 36*, 509–523.

Alwitt, L. F., Anderson, D. R., Pugzles-Lorch, E., & Levin, S. R. (1980). Preschool children's visual attention to attributes of television. *Human Communication Research, 7*, 52–67.

Anderson, C. A., & Bushman, B. J. (2001). Effects of violent video games on aggressive behavior, aggressive cognition, aggressive affect, physiological arousal, and prosocial behavior: A meta-analytic review of the scientific literature. *Psychological Science, 12*(5), 353–359.

Anderson, C. A., & Dill, K. E. (2000). Video games and aggressive thoughts, feelings, and behavior in the laboratory and in life. *Journal of Personality and Social Psychology, 78*, 772–790.

Anderson, D. R., & Burns, J. (1991). Paying attention to television. In J. Bryant & D. Zillmann (Eds.), *Responding to the screen: Reception and reaction processes* (pp. 3–25). Hillsdale, NJ: Lawrence Erlbaum Associates.

Anderson, D. R., & Levin, S. R. (1976). Young children's attention to Sesame Street. *Child Development, 47*, 806–811.

Anderson, D. R., & Pugzles-Lorch, E. (1983). Looking at television: Action or reaction. In J. Bryant & D. Anderson (Eds.), *Children's understanding of television* (pp. 1–33). New York: Academic Press.

Anderson, D. R., Pugzles-Lorch, E. P., Field, D. E., Collins, P. A., & Nathan, J. G. (1986). Television viewing at home: Age trends in visual attention and time with TV. *Child Development, 57*, 1024–1033.

Anderson, D. R., Pugzles-Lorch, E. P., Field, D. E., & Sanders, J. (1981). The effects of TV program comprehensibility on preschool children's visual attention to television. *Child Development, 52*, 151–157.

Anderson, J. C., Williams, S., McGee, R., & Silva, P. A. (1987). DSM-III disorders in preadolescent children. *Archives of General Psychiatry, 44*, 69–76.

Ankersmit, L., & Veen, J. (1995). *Special moves: Gebruik en betekenis van videospellen.* [Special moves: Use and meanings of video games]. Unpublished master's thesis. Department of Communication, University of Amsterdam.

Ariès, P. (1962). *Centuries of childhood: A social history of family life.* New York: Vintage Books.

Astington, J. W. (1993). *The child's discovery of the mind.* Cambridge, MA: Harvard University Press.

Atkin, C. K. (1975a). *First year of experimental evidence: The effects of television advertising on children, Report 1.* East Lansing, MI: Michigan State University. (ERIC Document Reproduction Service No. ED116783)

Atkin, C. K. (1975b). *Second year of experimental evidence: The effects of television advertising on children, Report 2.* East Lansing, MI: Michigan State University. (ERIC Document Reproduction Service No. ED116784)

Atkin, C. K. (1975c). *Survey of pre-adolescent's responses to television commercials: The effects of television advertising on children, Report 6.* East Lansing, MI: Michigan State University. (ERIC Document Reproduction Service No. ED116820)

Atkin, C. K. (1975d). *Survey of children's and mother's responses to television commercials: The effects of television advertising on children, Report 8.* East Lansing, MI: Michigan State University. (ERIC Document Reproduction Service No. ED123675)

Atkin, C. K. (1978). Observation of parent-child interaction in supermarket decision-making. *Journal of Marketing, 42,* 41–45.

Atkin, C. K., & Block, M. (1983). Effectiveness of celebrity endorsers. *Journal of Advertising Research, 32*(1), 57–61.

Badinand-Hubert, N., Mureau, M., Hirsch, E., Masnou, P., Nahum, L., Parain, D., & Naquet, R. (1998). Epilepsies and video games: Results of a multicentric study. *Electroencyphalography and Clinical Neurophysiology, 107*(6), 422–477.

Bandura, A. (1965). Influence of model's reinforcement contingencies on the acquisition of imitative responses. *Journal of Personality and Social Psychology, 1,* 589–595.

Bandura, A. (1973). *Aggression: A social learning analysis.* Englewood Cliffs, NJ: Prentice-Hall.

Bandura, A. (1986). *Social foundations of thought and action: A social cognitive theory.* Englewood Cliffs, NJ: Prentice-Hall.

Bandura, A. (1994). Social cognitive theory of mass communication. In J. Bryant & D. Zillmann (Eds.), *Media effects* (pp. 61–90). Hillsdale, NJ: Lawrence Erlbaum Associates.

Bauer, D. H. (1976). An exploratory study of developmental changes in children's fears. *Journal of Child Psychology and Psychiatry, 17,* 69–74.

Berkowitz, L. (1984). Some effects of thoughts on anti-social and prosocial influences of media effects: A cognitive-neoassociation analysis. *Psychological Bulletin, 95,* 410–427.

Berkowitz, L., & Alioto, J. T. (1973). The meaning of an observed event as a determinant of its aggressive consequences. *Journal of Personality and Social Psychology, 28,* 206–221.

Berkowitz, L., & Powers, P. C. (1979). Effects of timing and justification of witnessed aggression on the observers' punitiveness. *Journal of Research in Personality, 13,* 71–80.

Berlyne, D. E. (1971). *Aesthetics and psychobiology.* New York: Appleton-Century-Crofts.

Bickham, D. S., Wright, J. C., & Huston, A. C. (2001). Attention, comprehension, and the educational influences of television. In D. G. Singer & J. L. Singer (Eds.), *Handbook of children and the media* (pp. 101–120). Thousand Oaks, CA: Sage.

Boush, D. M. (2001). Mediating advertising effects. In J. Bryant & J. A. Bryant (Eds.), *Television and the American family* (pp. 397–414). Hillsdale, NJ: Lawrence Erlbaum Associates.

Bruner, J. S. (1966). On cognitive growth I & II. In J. S. Bruner, R. R. Oliver, & P. M. Greenfield (Eds.), *Studies in cognitive growth* (pp. 1–67). New York: John Wiley.

Bryant, J., Zillmann, D., & Brown, D. (1983). Entertainment features in children's educational television: Effects on attention and information acquisition. In J. Bryant & D. Anderson (Eds.), *Children's understanding of television* (pp. 221–240). New York: Academic Press.

Buckingham, D. (2000). *After the death of childhood: Growing up in the age of electronic media.* Cambridge, UK: Polity Press.

Buijzen, M., & Valkenburg, P. M. (2000a). Television commercials and children's toy wishes. *Journal of Broadcasting and Electronic Media, 44,* 456–469.

Buijzen, M., & Valkenburg, P. M. (2002b). Appeals in advertising aimed at children and adolescents. *Communications: The European Journal of Communications Research, 27,* 349–364.

Buijzen, M., & Valkenburg, P. M. (2003a). The effects of television advertising on materialism, parent–child conflict, and unhappiness: A review of research. *Journal of Applied Developmental Psychology, 24,* 437–456.

Buijzen, M., & Valkenburg, P. M. (2003b). The unintended effects of advertising: A parent–child survey. *Communication Research, 30,* 483–503.

Bushman, B. J. (1998). Priming effects of media violence on the accessibility of aggressive constructs in memory. *Personality and Social Psychology Bulletin, 24*(5), 537–545.

Bushman, B. J., & Huesmann, L. R. (2001). Effects of televised violence on aggression. In D. Singer & J. L. Singer (Eds.), *Handbook of children and the media* (pp. 223–254). Thousand Oaks, CA: Sage.

Calvert, S. L., Huston, A. C., Watkins, B. A., & Wright, J. C. (1982). The relationship between selective attention to television forms and children's comprehension of content. *Child Development, 53,* 601–610.

Campbell, T. A., Wright, J. C., & Huston, A. C. (1987). Form cues and content difficulty as determinants of children's cognitive processing of televised educational messages. *Journal of Experimental Child Psychology, 43,* 311–327.

Cantor, J. (1991). Fright responses to mass media productions. In J. Bryant & D. Zillmann (Eds.), *Responding to the screen* (pp. 169–197). Hillsdale, NJ: Lawrence Erlbaum Associates.

Cantor, J. (1998a). *Mommy I'm scared: How TV and movies frighten children and what we can do to protect them.* San Diego, CA: Harcourt Brace.

Cantor, J. (1998b). Children's attraction to violent television programming. In J. Goldstein (Ed.), *Attractions of violence* (pp. 88–115). New York: Oxford University Press.

Cantor, J. (2002). Fright reactions to mass media. In J. Bryant & D. Zillmann (Eds.), *Media effects* (pp. 287–306). Hillsdale, NJ: Lawrence Erlbaum Associates.

Cantor, J., & Nathanson, A. I. (1996). Children's fright reactions to television news. *Journal of Communication, 46,* 139–152.

Cantor, J., & Sparks, G. G. (1984). Children's fear responses to mass media: Testing some Piagetian predictions. *Journal of Communication, 34,* 90–103.

Cantor, J., Wilson, B. J., & Hoffner, C. (1986). Emotional responses to a televised nuclear holocaust film. *Communication Research, 13,* 257–277.

Cantril, H. (1940). *The invasion from Mars: A study in the psychology of panic.* Princeton, NJ: Princeton University Press.

Clavadetscher, J. E., Brown, A. M., Ankrum, C., & Teller, D. Y. (1988). Spectral sensitivity and chromatic discriminations in 3- and 7-week-old human infants. *Journal of the Optical Society of America, 5,* 2093–2105.

Clements, D. H. (1991). Enhancement of creativity in computer environments. *American Educational Research Journal, 28*(1), 173–187.

Cohen, J. (1988). *Statistical power analysis for the behavioral sciences* (2nd ed.). Hillsdale, NJ: Lawrence Erlbaum Associates.

Cohen, L. B. (1972). Attention-getting and attention-holding processes of infant visual preference. *Child Development, 43*, 869–879.

Collins, W. A. (1975). The developing child as a viewer. *Journal of Communication, 25*, 35–44.

Constanzo, P. R., & Shaw, M. E. (1966). Conformity as a function of age level. *Child Development, 37*, 967–975.

Cook, T. D., & Campbell, D. T. (1979). *Quasi-experimentation: Design and analysis issues for field settings.* Chicago: Rand McNally.

Corder-Bolz, C. R. (1980). Mediation: The role of significant others. *Journal of Communication, 30*(3), 106–108.

Cunningham, H. (1995). *Children and childhood in Western society since 1500.* London: Wesley Longman.

Cupitt, M., Jenkinson, D., Ungerer, J., & Waters, B. (1998). *Infants and television.* Sidney, Australia: Australian Broadcasting Authority.

Davidson, S. D. (1999). Cyber-cookies: How much should the public swallow? In D. Shumann & S. Thorson (Eds.), *Advertising and the World Wide Web* (pp. 219–232). Mahwah, NJ: Lawrence Erlbaum Associates.

Davies, H., Buckingham, D., & Kelley, P. (2000). In the worst possible taste: Children, television and cultural value. *European Journal of Cultural Studies, 3*(1), 5–25.

Davies, M. M. (1997). *Fake, fact, and fantasy: Children's interpretations of television reality.* Hillsdale, NJ: Lawrence Erlbaum Associates.

de Bruin, J. (1999). *De spanning van seksualiteit: Plezier en gevaar in jongerenbladen* [The suspense of sexuality: Pleasure and danger in youth magazines]. Amsterdam: Het Spinhuis.

Derbaix, C., & Bree, J. (1997). The impact of children's affective reactions elicited by commercials on attitudes toward the advertisement and the brand. *International Journal of Research in Marketing, 14*, 207–229.

Derscheid, L. E., Kwon, Y. H., & Fang, S. (1996). Preschoolers' socialization as consumers of clothing and recognition of symbolism. *Perceptual and Motor Skills, 82*, 1171–1181.

Dietz, T. L. (1998). An examination of violence and gender role portrayals in video games: Implications for gender socialization and aggressive behavior. *Sex Roles, 38*(5/6), 425–442.

Dollard, J., Miller, N. E., Doob, L. W., Mowrer, O. H., & Sears, R. H. (1939). *Frustration and aggression.* New Haven, CT: Yale University Press.

Dominick, J. R. (1984). Videogames, television violence, and aggression in teenagers. *Journal of Communication, 34*, 136–147.

Dubow, J. S. (1995). Advertising recognition and recall by age—including teens. *Journal of Advertising Research, 35*(5), 55–60.

Egli, E. A., & Meyers, L. S. (1984). The role of video game playing in adolescent life: Is there a reason to be concerned? *Bulletin of the Psychonomic Society, 22*, 209–312.

Elkind, D. (1981). *The hurried child: Growing up too fast too soon.* Reading, MA: Addison-Wesley.

Fagot, B. I. (1994). Peer relations and the development of competence in boys and girls. *New Directions for Child Development, 65*, 53–65.

Fein, G. G. (1981). Pretend play in childhood: An integrated review. *Child Development, 52*, 1095–1118.

Fernald, A. (1985). Four-month-old infants prefer to listen to motherese. *Infant Behavior and Development, 8*, 181–196.

Fernie, D. E. (1981). Ordinary and extraordinary people: Children's understanding of television and real life models. In H. Kelly & H. Gardner (Eds.), Viewing children through television. *New directions in Child Development, 13*, 47–58.

Feshbach, S. (1976). The role of fantasy in response to television. *Journal of Social Issues, 32*(4), 71–86.

Fischer, P. M., Schwartz, M. P., Richards, J. W., Goldstein, A. O., & Rojas, T. H. (1991). Brand logo recognition by children aged 3 to 6 years. *JAMA, 266,* 3145–3148.

Flavell, J. H., Miller, P., & Miller, S. A. (1993). *Cognitive development.* Englewood Cliffs, NJ: Prentice-Hall.

Flynn, J. R. (1987). Massive IQ gains in 14 nations: What IQ tests really measure. *Psychological Bulletin, 101,* 171–191.

Flynn, J. R. (1999). Searching for justice: The discovery of IQ gains over time. *American Psychologist, 54*(1), 5–20.

Fowles, J. (1999). *The case for media violence.* Thousand Oaks, CA: Sage.

Fraiberg, S. H. (1959). *The magic years: Understanding and handling the problems of early childhood.* New York: Charles Scribner's Sons.

Freedman, J. L. (1984). Effect of television violence on aggressiveness. *Psychological Bulletin, 96,* 227–246.

Frijda, N. H. (1988). The laws of emotion. *American Psychologist, 43,* 349–358.

Frijda, N. H. (1989). Aesthetic emotions and reality. *American Psychologist, 44,* 1546–1547.

Frijda, N. H. (2001). The laws of emotion. In W. G. Parrott (Ed.), *Emotions in social psychology* (pp. 57–70). Ann Arbor, MI: Edwards Brothers.

Fritz, J. (1995). *Warum computerspiele faszinieren: Empirische Annäherungen an Nutzung und Wirkung von Bildschirmspiele.* Weinheim: Juventa Verlag.

Gagnon, D. (1985). Videogames and spatial skills. *Educational Communication and Technology, 33,* 263–275.

Galst, J. P., & White, M. A. (1976). The unhealthy persuader: The reinforcing value of television and children's purchase-influencing attempts at the supermarket. *Child Development, 47,* 1089–1096.

Ganchrow, J. R., Steiner, J. E., & Daher, M. (1983). Neonatal facial expressions to different qualities and intensities of gustatory stimulation. *Infant Behavior and Development, 6,* 189–200.

Geen, R. G., & Rakosky, J. J. (1973). Interpretations of observed aggression and their effects on GSR. *Journal of Experimental Research in Personality, 25,* 289–292.

Gerbner, G. (1992, December). Testimony at hearings on violence on television before the House Judiciary Committee, Subcommittee on Crime and Criminal Justice, New York (field hearing).

Gerbner, G., Gross, L., Morgan, M., & Signorielli, N. (1994). Growing up with television: The cultivation perspective. In J. Bryant & D. Zillmann (Eds.), *Media effects: Advances in theory and research* (pp. 17–42). Hillsdale, NJ: Lawrence Erlbaum Associates.

Ghesquiere, R. (1988). *Het verschijnsel jeugdliteratuur* [The phenomenon of children's literature]. Leuven, Belgium: Acco.

Giroux, H. (1998). Are Disney movies good for your kids? In S. Steinberg & J. Kincheloe (Eds.), *Kinderculture: The corporate construction of childhood* (pp. 53–68). Boulder, CO: Westview.

Goldberg, M. E. (1990). A quasi-experiment assessing the effectiveness of TV advertising directed to children. *Journal of Marketing Research, 27,* 445–454.

Goldberg, M. E., & Gorn, G. J. (1978). Some unintended consequences of TV advertising to children. *Journal of Consumer Research, 5*(1), 22–29.

Goldstein, J. H. (1998). *Why we watch: The attractions of violent entertainment.* New York: Oxford University Press.

Gorn, G. J., & Florsheim, R. (1985). The effects of commercials for adult products on children. *Journal of Consumer Research, 11,* 962–967.

Gorn, G. J., & Goldberg, M. E. (1977). The impact of television advertising on children from low-income families. *Journal of Consumer Research, 4*, 86–88.

Gorn, G. J., & Goldberg, M. E. (1980). Children's responses to repetitive television commercials. *Journal of Consumer Research, 6*, 421–424.

Graf, W. D., Chatrian, G. E., Glass, S. T., & Knauss, T. A. (1994). Video game-related seizures: A report on 10 patients and a review of the literature. *Pediatrics, 93*(4), 551–556.

Green, C. S., & Bavelier, D. (2003). Action video game modifies visual selective attention. *Nature, 423*, 534–537.

Greenfield, P. M. (1984). *Mind and media: The effects of television, computers and video games.* Cambridge, MA: Harvard University Press.

Greenfield, P. M. (1998). The cultural evolution of IQ. In U. Neisser (Ed.), *The rising curve: Long-term gains in IQ and related measures* (pp. 81–123). Washington, DC: American Psychological Association.

Greenfield, P. M., Brannon, C., & Lohr, D. (1994). Two-dimensional representation of movement through three-dimensional space: The role of video game expertise. *Journal of Applied Developmental Psychology, 15*, 87–103.

Greenfield, P. M., de Winstanley, P., Kilpatric, H., & Kaye, D. (1994). Action video games and informal education: Effects on strategies for dividing visual attention. *Journal of Applied Developmental Psychology, 15*, 105–123.

Griffith, J. L., Voloschin, P., Gibb, G. D., & Bailey, J. R. (1983). Differences in eye-hand motor coordination of video-game users and non-users. *Perceptual & Motor Skills, 69*, 243–247.

Griffiths, M. D. (1998). Dependence on computer games by adolescents. *Psychological Reports, 82*, 475–480.

Griffiths, M. D., & Hunt, N. (1995). Computer game playing in adolescence: Prevalence and demographic indicators. *Journal of Community and Applied Social Psychology, 5*, 189–193.

Grodal, T. (2000). Video games and the pleasures of control. In D. Zillmann & P. Vorderer (Eds.), *Media entertainment: The psychology of its appeal* (pp. 197–214). Mahwah, NJ: Lawrence Erlbaum Associates.

Gullone, E. (2000). The development of normal fear: A century of research. *Clinical Psychology Review, 20*, 429–451.

Gunter, B., & Furnham, A. (1984). Perceptions of television violence: Effects of programme genre and type of violence on viewers' judgments of violent portrayals. *British Journal of Social Psychology, 23*, 155–164.

Gunter, B., McAleer, J., & Clifford, B. R. (1991). *Children's view about television.* Aldershot, UK: Avebury Academic Publishing Group.

Hall, J., Shaw, M., Johnson, M., & Oppenheim, P. (1995). Influence of children on family consumer decision making. *European Advances in Consumer Research, 2*, 45–53.

Harris, P. L. (2000). *Understanding children's worlds: The work of the imagination.* Oxford, UK: Blackwell.

Heath, L. (1984). Impact of newspaper crime reports on fear of crime: Multimethodological investigation. *Journal of Personality and Social Psychology, 47*, 263–276.

Heeter, C. (1988). Gender differences in viewing styles. In C. Heeter & B. Greenberg (Eds.), *Cableviewing.* Norwood, NJ: Ablex.

Henke, L. L. (1999). Children, advertising and the Internet: An exploratory study. In D. Shumann & E. Thorson (Eds.), *Advertising and the World Wide Web* (pp. 73–79). Mahwah, NJ: Lawrence Erlbaum Associates.

Heslop, L. A., & Ryans, A. B. (1980). A second look at children and the advertising of premiums. *Journal of Consumer Research, 6*, 414–420.

Hicks, D. J. (1965). Imitation and retention of film-mediated aggressive peer and adult models. *Journal of Personality and Social Psychology, 2*, 97–100.

Himmelweit, H. T., Oppenheim, A. N., & Vince, P. (1958). *Television and the child: An empirical study of the effect of television on the young.* London, UK: Oxford University Press.

Hite, C. R., & Hite, R. E. (1995). Reliance on brand by young children. *Journal of the Marketing Research Society, 37*(2), 185–193.

Hoekstra, S. J., Harris, R. J., & Helmick, A. L. (1999). Autobiographical memories about the experience of seeing frightening movies in childhood. *Media Psychology, 1*, 117–140.

Hoffman, M. L. (2000). *Empathy and moral development: Implications for caring and justice.* Cambridge, UK: Cambridge University Press.

Hoffner, C., & Cantor, J. (1985). Developmental differences in children's responses to a television character's appearance and behavior. *Developmental Psychology, 21*, 1065–1074.

Hoffner, C., & Cantor, J. (1991). Perceiving and responding to mass media characters. In J. Bryant & D. Zillmann (Eds.), *Responding to the screen: Reception and reaction processes* (pp. 63–102). Hillsdale, NJ: Lawrence Erlbaum Associates.

Holden, G. W. (1983). Avoiding conflict: Mothers as tacticians in de supermarket. *Child Development, 54*, 233–240.

Hovland, C., & Weiss, W. (1951). The influence of source credibility on communication effectiveness. *Public Opinion Quarterly, 15*, 635–650.

Howard, S. (1998). Unbalanced minds? Children thinking about television. In S. Howard (Ed.), *Wired-up: Young people and the electronic media* (pp. 57–76). London: UCL Press.

Huesmann, L. R., Moise-Titus, J., Podolski, C. L., & Eron, L. D. (2003). Longitudinal relations between children's exposure to TV violence and their aggressive and violent behavior in young adulthood: 1977–1992. *Developmental Psychology, 39*, 201–221.

Husson, W. (1982). Theoretical issues in the study of children's attention to television. *Communication Research, 9*, 323–351.

Huston, A. C., & Wright, J. C. (1983). Children's processing of television: The informative functions of formal features. In J. Bryant & D. Anderson (Eds.), *Children's understanding of TV: Research on attention and comprehension* (pp. 37–68). New York: Academic Press.

Huston, A. C., Wright, J. C., Rice, M. L., Kerkman, D., & St. Peters, M. (1990). Development of television viewing patterns in early childhood: A longitudinal investigation. *Developmental Psychology, 26*, 409–420.

Isler, L., Popper, E. T., & Ward, S. (1987). Children's purchase requests and parental responses: Results from a diary study. *Journal of Advertising Research, 27*(5), 29–39.

Jaglom, L. M., & Gardner, H. (1981). The preschool viewer as anthropologist. In H. Kelly, & H. Gardner (Eds.), Viewing children through television. *New directions in Child Development, 13*, 9–29.

James, N. C., & McCain, T. A. (1982). Television games preschool children play: Patterns, themes and uses. *Journal of Broadcasting, 26*, 783–800.

Jo, E., & Berkowitz, L. (1994). A priming effect analysis of media influences: An update. In J. Bryant & D. Zillmann (Eds.), *Media effects* (pp. 43–60). Hillsdale, NJ: Lawrence Erlbaum Associates.

Johnson, J. G., Smailes, E. M., Kasen, S., & Brook, J. S. (2002). Television viewing and aggressive behavior during adolescence and adulthood. *Science, 295*(5564), 2468–2471.

Johnston, D. D. (1995). Adolescents' motivations for viewing graphic horror. *Human Communication Research, 231*, 522–552.

Joy, L. A., Kimball, M. M., & Zabrack, M. L. (1986). Television and children's aggressive behavior. In T. M. Williams (Ed.), *The impact of television: A natural experiment in three communities* (pp. 303–360). Orlando, FL: Academic Press.

Kail, J. E. (1995). A history of children's books publishing. *Journal of Youth Services in Libraries, 8,* 259–266.

Karl, J. E. (1995). A history of children's books publishing. *Journal of Youth Services in Libraries, 8,* 259–266.

Keij, M. (1995). *C'est plus fort que toi.* Unpublished master's thesis. Department of Communication Science, University of Amsterdam.

Kellner, D. (1998). Beavis and Butt-Head: No future for postmodern youth. In S. Steinberg & J. L. Kincheloe (Eds.), *Kinderculture: The corporate construction of childhood* (pp. 85–102). Boulder, CO: Westview Press.

Kiesler, S., Siegel, J., & McGuire, T. W., (1984). Social psychological aspects of computer-mediated communication. *American Psychologist, 39,* 10, 1123–1134.

Kinder, M. (1991). *Playing with power in movies, television, and video games: From Muppet Babies to Teenage Mutant Ninja Turtles.* Berkeley, CA: University of California Press.

Kinder, M. (1996). Contextualizing video game violence: From Teenage Mutant Ninja Turtles 1 to Mortal Kombat 2. In P. M. Greenfield & R. R. Cocking (Eds.), *Interacting with video* (pp. 25–38). Norwood, NJ: Ablex Publishing.

Kinder, M. (1999). *Kids' media culture.* London: Duke University Press.

King, N. J., Gullone, E., & Ollendick, T. H. (1998). Etiology of childhood phobias: Current status of Rachman's three pathways theory. *Behaviour Research and Therapy, 36,* 297–309.

Kirby, L. (1988). Male hysteria and early cinema. *Camera Obscura, 17,* 112–131.

Klapper, J. T. (1960). *The effects of mass communication.* New York: Free Press.

Kraut, R., Kielser, S., Boneva, B., Cummings, J., Helgeson, V., & Crawford, A. (2002). Internet paradox revisited. *Journal of Social Issues, 58,* 49–74.

Kraut, R., Patterson, M., Lundmark, V., Kiesler, S., Mukopadhyay, T., & Scherlis, W. (1998). Internet paradox: A social technology that reduces social involvement and psychological well-being? *American Psychologist, 53*(9), 1017–1031.

Krcmar, M., & Valkenburg, P. M. (1999). A scale to assess children's moral interpretations of justified and unjustified violence and its relationship to television viewing. *Communication Research, 26,* 608–634.

Kubey, R., & Larson, R. (1990). The use and experience of the new video media among children and young adolescents. *Communication Research, 17,* 107–130.

Kuhlman, J. S., & Beitel, P. A. (1991). Videogame experience: A possible explanation for differences in anticipation of coincidence. *Perceptual and Motor Skills, 72,* 483–488.

Kunkel, D. (1988). Children and host-selling television commercials. *Communication Research, 15,* 71–92.

Lasswell, H. D. (1927). *Propaganda technique in the world war.* New York: Peter Smith.

Leaper, C. (1994). Exploring the consequences of gender segregation on social relationships: Causes and consequences. *New Directions for Child Development, 65,* 67–85.

Lemish, D. (1987). Viewers in diapers: The early development of television viewing. In T. R. Lindlof (Ed.), *Natural audiences: Qualitative research of media uses and effects* (pp. 33–57). Norwood, NJ: Ablex.

Lenhart, A., Rainie, L., & Lewis, O. (2001). *Teenage life online: The rise of the Instant-Message generation and the Internet's impact on friendships and family relations.* Washington, DC: Pew Internet & American Life Project. Retrieved February 2002 from www.pewinternet.org

Lesser, G. S. (1974). *Children and television: Lessons from Sesame Street.* New York: Random House.

Leyens, J. P., Camino, L., Parke, R. D., & Berkowitz, L. (1975). Effects of movie violence on aggression in a field setting as a function of group dominance and cohesion. *Journal of Personality and Social Psychology, 32,* 346–360.

Lin, S., & Lepper, M. (1987). Correlates of children's usage of video games and computers. *Journal of Applied Social Psychology, 17,* 72–93.

Linn, M. C., de Benedictis, T., & Delucchi, K. (1982). Adolescent reasoning about advertisements: Preliminary investigations. *Child Development, 53,* 1599–1633.

Linz, D. G., Donnerstein, E., & Penrod, S. (1984). The effects of multiple exposures to filmed violence against women. *Journal of Communication, 34*(3), 130–147.

Livingstone, S. (1998). *Making sense of television: The psychology of audience interpretation.* London: Routledge.

Locke, J. L. (1998). *The de-voicing of society: Why we don't talk to each other anymore.* New York: Simon & Schuster.

Loughlin, M., & Desmond, R. J. (1981). Social interaction in advertising directed to children. *Journal of Broadcasting, 25,* 303–307.

Luke, C. (1990). *TV and your child.* Sydney, Australia: Angus and Robertson.

Maccoby, E. E. (1951). Television: Its impact on school children. *Public Opinion Quarterly, 15,* 421–444.

Maccoby, E. E. (1988). Gender as a social category. *Developmental Psychology, 24,* 755–765.

Maccoby, E. E. (1990). Gender and Relationships: A developmental account. *American Psychologist, 45,* 513–520.

Macgregor, D. M. (2000). Nintendonitis? A case report of repetitive strain injury in a child as a result of playing computer games. *Scottish Medical Journal, 45*(5), 150.

Macklin, M. C. (1983). Do children understand TV ads? *Journal of Advertising Research, 23*(1), 63–70.

Macklin, M. C. (1994). The effects of an advertising retrieval cue on young children's memory and brand evaluations. *Psychology & Marketing, 11,* 291–311.

Macklin, M. C. (1996). Preschoolers' learning of brand names from visual cues. *Journal of Consumer Research, 23,* 251–261.

Mangleburg, T. F. (1990). Children's influence in purchase decisions: A review and critique. *Advances in Consumer Research, 17,* 813–825.

Martin, C. L. (1994). Cognitive influences on the development and maintenance of gender segregation. *New Directions for Child Development, 65,* 35–51.

Martin, M. C., & Kennedy, P. F. (1993). Advertising and social consequences for female preadolescents and adolescents. *Psychology & Marketing, 10,* 513–530.

Maurer, A. (1965). What children fear? *The Journal of Genetic Psychology, 106,* 265–277.

McCall, R. B., Kennedy, C. B., & Applebaum, M. I. (1977). Magnitude of discrepancy and the distribution of attention in infants. *Child Development, 48,* 772–86.

McCartney, K., & Rosenthal, R. (2000). Effect size, practical importance, and social policy for children. *Child Development, 71,* 173–180.

McGhee, P. E. (1979). *Humor: Its origin and development.* San Francisco: W. H. Freeman and Company.

McLaren, P., & Morris, J. (1998). Mighty Morphin Power Rangers: The aesthetics of phallomilitaristic justice. In S. Steinberg & J. L. Kincheloe (Eds.), *Kinderculture* (pp. 115–128). Boulder, CO: Westview Press.

McNeal, J. U. (1992). *Kids as customers: A handbook of marketing to children.* New York: Lexington Books.

McNeal, J. U. (1999). *The kids market: Myths and realities.* New York: Paramount Market Publishing.

Meigs, C. L. (1969). *A critical history of children's literature: A survey of children's books in English.* London: Macmillan.

Meyrowitz, J. (1985). *No sense of place: The impact of electronic media on social behavior.* New York: Oxford University Press.

Middelmann, A., & Melzer, B. (1984). The importance of brand preference in adolescence for brand loyalty later on—new answers to a fundamental question of youth marketing. *In Seminar on marketing to children and young consumers—Tactics for today, and strategies for tomorrow* (pp. 161–176). Nuerenberg, Germany: European Society for Opinion and Marketing Research.

Mielke, K. W. (1983). Formative research on appeal and comprehension in 3-2-1 contact. In J. Bryant & D. Anderson (Eds.), *Children's understanding of television: Research on attention and comprehension* (pp. 241–263). Hillsdale, NJ: Lawrence Erlbaum Associates.

Miller, J. H., & Busch, P. (1979). Host selling vs. premium TV commercials: An experimental evaluation of their influence on children. *Journal of Marketing Research, 16*, 323–332.

Mischel, H. N., & Mischel, W. (1983). The development of children's knowledge of self-control strategies. *Child Development, 53*, 603–619.

Mischel, W., & Ebbeson, E. B. (1970). Attention in delay of gratification. *Journal of Personality and Social Psychology, 16*, 329–337.

Mitchel, E. (1985). The dynamics of family interaction around home video games. *Marriage and the Family Review, 8*, 121–135.

Mitchel, K. J., Finkelhor, D., & Wolak, J. (2001). Risk factors for and impact of online sexual solicitation on youth. *JAMA, 285*, 3011–3014.

Mizerski, R. (1995). The relationship between cartoon trade character recognition and attitude toward product category in young children. *Journal of Marketing, 59*, 58–70.

Montgommery, K. (2000). Children's media culture in the new millennium: Mapping the digital landscape. *Future of the Children, 20*(2), 145–168.

Moog, H. (1976). The development of musical experience in preschool children. *Psychology of Music, 4*(2), 38–45.

Moore, E. S., & Lutz, R. J. (2000). Children, advertising, and product experiences: A multimethod inquiry. *Journal of Consumer Research 27*, 31–48.

Moschis, G. P., & Moore, R. L. (1981). A study of the acquisition of desires for products and brands. In K. Bernardt, I. Dolich, M. Etzel, W. Hehoe, T. Kinnear, W. Perreault, & K. Roering (Eds.), *The changing marketing environment: New theories and applications* (pp. 201–204). Chicago, IL: American Marketing Association.

Moschis, G. P., & Moore, R. L. (1982). A longitudinal study of television advertising effects. *Journal of Consumer Research, 9*, 279–286.

Muris, P., Merckelbach, H., & Collaris, R. (1997). Common childhood fears and their origins. *Behaviour Research and Therapy, 35*, 929–937.

Muris, P., Merckelbach, H., Gadet, B., & Moulaert, V. (2000). Fears, worries, and scary dreams in 4- to 12-year-old children: Their content, developmental pattern, and origins. *Journal of Clinical Child Psychology, 29*, 43–52.

Musgrave, F. (1966). *The family, education and society.* London: Routledge and Kegan Paul.

Nathanson, A. I. (1999). Identifying the relationship between parental mediation and children's aggression. *Communication Research, 26*, 124–144.

Nathanson, A. I., & Cantor, J. (2000). Reducing the aggression-promoting effect of violent cartoons by increasing children's fictional involvement with the victim: A study of active Mediation. *Journal of Broadcasting and Electronic Media, 44*, 125–142.

Neijens, P. (2000). *Verleidingskunsten op het raakvlak van voorlichting, commercie en vrije publiciteit: Inaugurele rede.* Amsterdam: Vossiuspers AUP.

Neisser, U. (1998). Using test scores and what they mean. In U. Neisser (Ed.), *The rising curve: Long-term gains in IQ and related measures* (pp. 3–22). Washington, DC: American Psychological Association.

Noble, G. (1975). *Children in front of the small screen.* Beverly Hills, CA: Sage.

Nomikos, M., Opton, E., Avetrill, J., & Lazarus, R. (1968). Surprise versus suspense in the production of stress reaction. *Journal of Personality and Social Psychology, 8*, 204–208.

NOP Research Group. (2001). *Girls catch boys as three-quarters of kids use Internet.* Retrieved September 2002 from http:/www.nop.co.uk

O'Brien, M., & Huston, A. C. (1985). Development of sex-typed play behavior in toddlers. *Developmental Psychology, 21*(5), 866–871.

Okagaki, L., & Frensch, P. A. (1994). Effects of video game playing on measures of spatial performance: Gender effects in late adolescents. *Journal of Applied Developmental Psychology, 15*, 33–58.

Ollendick, T. H., & King, N. J. (1991). Origins of childhood fears: An evaluation of Rachman's theory of fear acquisition. *Behaviour Research and Therapy, 29*, 117–123.

Osborn, D. K., & Endsley, R. C. (1971). Emotional reactions of young children to tv violence. *Child Development, 42*, 321–331.

Paik, H. (2001). The history of children's use of electronic media. In D. Singer & J. Singer (Eds.), *Handbook of children and the media* (pp. 7–28). Thousand Oaks, CA: Sage.

Paik, H., & Comstock, G. (1994). The effects of television violence on antisocial behavior: A meta-analysis. *Communication Research, 21*, 516–546.

Parker, J. (1995). Age differences in source monitoring of performed and imagined actions on immediate and delayed tests. *Journal of Experimental Child Psychology, 60*, 84–101.

Parks, M. R., & Roberts, L. D. (1998). 'Making MOOsic': The development of personal relationships on line and a comparison to their off-line counterparts. *Journal of Social and Personal Relationships, 15*(4), 517–537.

Peck, E. (1999). *Gender differences in film-induced fear as a function of type of emotion measure and stimulus content: A meta analysis and laboratory study.* Unpublished doctoral dissertation. University of Wisconsin, Madison.

Piaget, J. (1929). *The child's conception of the world.* London: Routledge & Kegan.

Piaget, J. (1954). *The construction of reality in the child.* New York: Basic Books.

Piaget, J. (1981). *Intelligence and affectivity: Their relationship during child development.* Palo Alto, CA: Annual Reviews.

Pingree, S. (1986). Children's activity and television comprehensibility. *Communication Research, 13*, 239–256.

Postman, N. (1983). *The disappearance of childhood.* London: W. H. Allen.

Provenzo, E. (1991). *Video kids: Making sense of Nintendo.* Cambridge, MA: Harvard University Press.

Pugzles-Lorch, E. P., Anderson, D. R., & Levin, S. R. (1979). The relationship of visual attention to children's comprehension of television. *Child Development, 50*, 722–727.

Putnam, R. (2000). *Bowling alone: The collapse and revival of American community.* New York: Simon & Schuster.

Rachman, S. J. (1991). Neoconditioning and the classical theory of fear acquisition. *Clinical Psychology Review, 11*, 155–173.

Rakow, L. (1988). Women and the telephone: The gendering of a communications technology. In C. Kramarae (Ed.), *Technology and women's voices: Keeping in touch* (pp. 207–229). New York: Routledge and Kegan Paul.

Rice, M. L., Huston, A. C., Truglio, A. C., & Wright, J. (1990). Words from "Sesame Street": Learning vocabulary while viewing. *Developmental Psychology, 26*, 421–428.

Richards, J., & Gibson, T. (1997). Extended visual fixation in young infants: Fixation distributions, heart rate changes, and attention. *Child Development, 68*, 1041–1056.

Richins, M. L. (1991). Social comparison and the idealized images of advertising. *Journal of Consumer Research, 18*, 71–83.

Riecken, G., & Ugur, Y. (1990). Children's general, product and brand-specific attitudes towards television commercials. *International Journal of Advertising, 9*, 136–148.

Roberts, D. F. (2000). Media and youth: Access, exposure and privatization. *Journal of Adolescent Health, 27*(2), 8–14.

Roberts, D. F., Foehr, U. G., Rideout, V. J., & Brodie, M. (1999). *Kids & media at the new millennium.* Menlo Park, CA: Kaiser Family Foundation.

Robertson, T. S., & Rossiter, J. R. (1976). Short-run advertising effects on children: A field study. *Journal of Marketing Research, 13*, 68–70.

Robertson, T. S., Rossiter, J. R., & Ward, S. (1985). Consumer satisfaction among children. *Advances in Consumer Research, 12,* 279–284.

Robertson, T. S., Ward, S., Gatignon, H., & Klees, D. M. (1989). Advertising and children: A cross-cultural study. *Communication Research, 16,* 459–485.

Roschelle, J. M., Pea, R. D., Hoadley, C. M., Gordin, D. N., & Means, B. M. (2000). Changing how and what children learn in school with computer-based technologies. *Future of Children, 10*(2), 76–101.

Rosengren, K. E., & Windahl, S. (1989). *Media matter: TV use in childhood and adolescence.* Norwood, NJ: Ablex.

Rosenthal, R., & Rubin, D. B. (1982). A simple, general purpose display of magnitude of experimental effect. *Journal of Educational Psychology, 74,* 166–169.

Ross, R. P., Campbell, T., Wright, J. C., Huston, A. C., Rice, M. L., & Turk, P. (1981). When celebrities talk, children listen: An experimental analysis of children's responses to TV ads with celebrity endorsement. *Journal of Applied Developmental Psychology, 5,* 185–202.

Ruff, H. A., & Lawson, K. R. (1990). Development of sustained focused attention in young children during free play. *Developmental Psychology, 26,* 85–93.

Ruff, H. A., & Rothbart, M. K. (1996). *Attention in early development: Themes and variations.* New York: Oxford University Press.

Sanger, J., Willson, J., Davis, B., & Whittaker, R. (1997). *Young children, videos and computer games: Issues for teachers and parents.* London: Falmer Press.

Sapolsky, B. S., & Molitor, F. (1996). Content trends in contemporary horror films. In J. B. Weaver & R. Tamborini (Eds.), *Horror films: Current research on audience preferences and reactions* (pp. 33–48). Mahwah, NJ: Lawrence Erlbaum Associates.

Sapolsky, B. S., & Zillmann, D. (1978). Experience and empathy: Affective reactions to witnessing child-birth. *Journal of Social Psychology, 105,* 131–144.

Sarafino, E. P. (1986). *The fears of childhood.* New York: Human Science Press.

Schramm, W., Lyle, J., & Parker, E. (1961). *Television in the lives of children.* Stanford, CA: Stanford University Press.

Seiter, E. (1998). Children's desires/Mothers dilemmas: The social context of consumption. In H. Jenkins (Ed.), *The children's culture reader* (pp. 297–317). New York: New York University Press.

Selman, R. L. (1980). *The growth of interpersonal understanding.* New York: Academic Press.

Severin, W. J., & Tankard, J. W. (1997). *Communication theories: Origins, methods, and uses in the mass media: Fourth edition.* White Plains, NY: Longman.

Sheldon, L. (1998). Children and television: Cool or just plain boring. In S. Howard (Ed.), *Wired-up: Young people and the electronic media* (pp. 77–94). London, UK: UCL Press Ltd.

Sheldon, L., & Loncar, M. (1996). *Kids talk TV: 'Super wicked' or 'dum'.* Sidney, Australia: Australian Broadcasting Authority.

Sherry, J. (2001). The effects of violent video games on aggression? A meta-analysis. *Human Communication Research, 27,* 409–431.

Shimp, T. A., Dyer, R. F., & Devita, S. F. (1976). An experimental test of the harmful effects of premium-oriented commercials. *Journal of Consumer Research, 3,* 1–11.

Siegler, R. S. (1998). *Children's thinking* (3rd ed.). Englewood Cliffs, NJ: Prentice Hall.

Singer, J. L. (1980). The power and limitations of television: A cognitive-affective analysis. In P. H. Tannenbaum & R. Abeles (Eds.), *The entertainment functions of television* (pp. 31–65). Hillsdale, NJ: Lawrence Erlbaum Associates.

Singer, J. L., & Singer, D. G. (1976). Can TV stimulate imaginative play? *Journal of Communication, 26*(3), 75–80.

Smith, S., & Wilson, B. J. (2000). Children's reactions to a television news story: The impact of video footage and proximity of the crime. *Communication Research, 27,* 641–673.

Sparks, G. G. (1986). Developmental differences in children's reports of fear induced by the mass media. *Child Study Journal, 16,* 55–66.

Sparks, G. G., & Sparks, C. W. (2000). Violence, mayhem, and horror. In D. Zillmann & P. Vorderer (Eds.), *Media entertainment: The psychology of its appeal* (pp. 73–92). Mahwah, NJ: Lawrence Erlbaum Associates.

Stoneman, Z., & Brody, G. H. (1983). Immediate and long-term recognition and generalization of advertised products as a function of age and presentation mode. *Developmental Psychology, 19,* 56–61.

Stotland, E. (1969). Exploratory investigations of empathy. In L. Berkowitz (Ed.), *Advances in experimental social psychology* (pp. 271–314). New York: Academic Press.

Subrahmanyam, K., & Greenfield, P. M. (1998). Computer games for girls: What makes them play? In J. Cassell & H. Jenkins (Eds.), *From Barbie to Mortal Kombat: Gender and computer games* (pp. 46–71). Cambridge, MA: MIT press.

Subrahmanyan, K., Greenfield, P., Kraut, R., & Gross, E. F. (2001). The impact of computer use on children's and adolescents' development. *Journal of Applied Developmental Psychology, 22*(1), 7–30.

Sullivan, H. S. (1953). *The interpersonal theory of psychiatry.* New York: Norton.

Tamborini, R., & Weaver, J. (1996). Frightening entertainment: A historical perspective of fictional horror. In J. B. Weaver & R. Tamborini (Eds.), *Horror films: Current research on audience preferences and reactions* (pp. 1–14). Mahwah, NJ: Lawrence Erlbaum Associates.

Thayer, J. F., & Levinson, R. W. (1983). Effects of music on psychophysiological responses to a stressful film. *Psychomusicology, 3,* 44–52.

Thomas, M. H., Horton, R. W., Lippincott, E. C., & Drabman, R. S. (1977). Desensitization to portrayals of real-life aggression as a function of exposure to television violence. *Journal of Personality and Social Psychology, 35,* 450–458.

Thompson, K. M., & Haninger, K. (2001). Violence in e-rated video games. *JAMA, 286*(5), 591–597.

Tobin, J. (2000). *Good guys don't wear hats: Children's talk about the media.* New York: Teachers College Press.

Turow, J. (2001). Family boundaries, commercialism, and the Internet: A framework for research. *Journal of Applied Developmental Psychology, 22,* 73–86.

Turow, J., & Nir, L. (2000). *The Internet and the family 2000: The view from parents, the view from kids.* Washington DC: The Annenberg Public Policy Center.

Ullian, D. Z. (1977). The development of conceptions of masculinity and femininity. *Dissertation Abstracts International, 37*(7-B), 3590.

U.S. Census Bureau. (2001). 9-in-10 school-age children have computer access. Retrieved October 2001 from http://www.census.gov/press-release

Valkenburg, P. M. (1999). De ontwikkeling van kind tot consument [The development of a child into a consumer]. *Tijdschrift voor Communicatiewetenschap, 27,* 30–46.

Valkenburg, P. M. (2001). Television and children's developing imagination. In D. Singer & J. Singer (Eds.), *Handbook of research on children and the media* (pp. 121–134). Thousand Oaks, CA: Sage.

Valkenburg, P. M., & Buijzen, M. (2003). Children, computer games, and the Internet. *Netherlands Journal of Social Sciences, 3g*(1), 24–34.

Valkenburg, P. M., & Cantor, J. (2000). Children's likes and dislikes of entertainment programs. In D. Zillmann & P. Vorderer (Eds.), *Media entertainment: The psychology of its appeal* (pp. 135–152). Mahwah, NJ: Lawrence Erlbaum Associates.

Valkenburg, P. M., & Cantor, J. (2001). The development of a child into a consumer. *Journal of Applied Developmental Psychology, 22,* 61–72.

Valkenburg, P. M., Cantor, J., & Peeters, A. L. (2000). Fright reactions to television: A Child Survey. *Communication Research, 27,* 82–99.

Valkenburg, P. M., & Janssen, S. C. (1999). What do children value in entertainment programs? A cross-cultural investigation. *Journal of Communication. 26,* 3–21.

Valkenburg, P. M., Krcmar, M., Peeters, A., & Marseille, N. M. (1999). Developing a scale to assess three styles of television mediation: "restrictive mediation," "instructive mediation," and "social coviewing." *Journal of Broadcasting and Electronic Media, 43,* 52–66.

Valkenburg, P. M., & Soeters, K. (2001). Children's positive and negative experiences with the Internet. *Communication Research, 28,* 653–676.

Valkenburg, P. M., Walma van der Molen, J., & Peeters, A. L. (2001). Should news on child homicides be broadcast? Opinions of parents, teachers, and children. *Communications: The European Journal of Communications Research, 26,* 229–245.

Valkenburg, P. M., & Van Wijnbergen, C. (2002). Merklogoherinnering bij vier- tot negenjarige kinderen [Brand logo recall among 4- to 9-year-olds]. *Tijdschrift voor Communicatiewetenschap, 30,* 7–17.

Valkenburg, P. M., & Vroone, M. (2004). Developmental changes in infants' and toddlers' attention to television entertainment. *Communication Research, 31.*

Van der Voort, T. H. A. (1997). *De invloed van televisiegeweld* [The influence of television violence]. Amsterdam/Lisse, The Netherlands: Swets & Zeitlinger.

Van Schie, E., Wiegman, O., Kuttschreuter, M., & Boer, H. (1996). Speelfrequentie, vrijetijdsbesteding en sociale integratie bij computerspelen. *Tijdschrift voor Communicatiewetenschap, 24,* 29-39.

Venn, J. R., & Short, J. G. (1973). Vicarious classical conditioning of emotional responses in nursery school children. *Journal of Personality and Social Psychology, 28,* 249–255.

Walker, J. R., & Bellamy, R. V. (2001). Remote control devices and family viewing. In J. Bryant & J. A. Bryant (Eds.), *Television and the American family* (pp. 75–90). Mahwah, NJ: Lawrence Erlbaum Associates.

Walma van der Molen, J. H., Valkenburg, P. M., & Peeters, A. L. (2002). Television news and fears: A child survey. *Communications: The European Journal of Communications Research, 27,* 303–317.

Walters, K. S. (1989). The law of apparent reality and aesthetic emotions. *American Psychologist, 44,* 1545–1546.

Walther, J. G., Anderson, J. F., & Park, D. W. (1994). Interpersonal effects in computer-mediated interaction: A meta-analysis of social and antisocial communication. *Communication Research, 21,* 460–487.

Ward, S., & Wackman, D. B. (1971). Family and media influences on adolescent consumer learning. *American Behavioral Scientist, 14,* 415–427.

Ward, S., & Wackman, D. B. (1972). Children's purchase influence attempts and parental yielding. *Journal of Marketing Research, 9,* 316–319.

Wartella, E., & Ettema, J. S. (1974). A cognitive developmental study of children's attention to television commercials. *Communication Research, 1,* 46–49.

Watts, J. H., & Welch, A. J. (1983). Effects of static and dynamic complexity on children's attention and recall of televised instruction. In J. Bryant & D. Anderson (Eds.), *Children's understanding of television* (pp. 69–102). New York: Academic Press.

Weiss, B. W., Katkin, E. S., & Rubin, B. M. (1968). Relationship between a factor analytically derived measure of a specific fear and performance after related fear induction. *Journal of Abnormal Psychology, 73,* 461–463.

Wellman, H. M. (1990). *The child's theory of mind.* Cambridge, MA: Bradford Books/MIT Press.

Williams, L. A., & Burns, A. C. (2000). Exploring the dimensionality of children's direct influence attempts. *Advances in Consumer Research, 27,* 64–71.

Wilson, B., Kunkel, D., Linz, D., Potter, J., Donnerstein, E., Smith, S., Blumenthal, E., & Berry, M. (1998). Violence in Television programming overall. In Center for Communication and Social Policy (Ed.), *National Television Violence Study 2* (pp. 4–204). Thousand Oaks, CA: Sage.

Wilson, B. J., & Weiss, A. J. (1992). Developmental differences in children's reactions to a toy advertisement linked to a toy-based cartoon. *Journal of Broadcasting & Electronic Media, 36,* 371–394.

Wolak, J., Mitchell, K. J., & Finkelhor, D. (2002). Close online relationships in a national sample of adolescents. *Adolescence, 37,* 441–455.

Wood, W., Wong, F. Y., & Chachere, J. G. (1991). Effects of media violence on viewers aggression in unconstrained social interaction. *Psychological Bulletin, 109,* 371–383.

Woodard, E. H., & Gridina, N. (2000). *Media in the home 2000: The fifth annual survey of parents and children.* Washington, DC: Annenberg Public Policy Center.

Wotring, C. E., & Greenberg, B. S. (1973). Experiments in televised violence and verbal aggression: Two exploratory studies. *Journal of Communication, 23,* 446–460.

Wright, J. C., Huston, A. C., Reitz, A. L., & Piemyat, S. (1994). Young children's perceptions of television reality: Determinants and developmental differences. *Developmental Psychology, 30,* 229–239.

Wright, J. C., St. Peters, M., & Huston, A. C. (1990). Family television use and its relation to children's cognitive skills and social behavior. In J. Bryant (Ed.), *Television and the American family* (pp. 227–252). Hillsdale, NJ: Lawrence Erlbaum Associates.

Young, B. (1990). *Television advertising and children.* Oxford, UK: Clarendon Press.

Zillmann, D. (1978). Attribution and misattribution of excitatory reactions. In J. H. Harvey, W. Ickes, & R. F. Kidd (Eds.), *New directions in attribution research* (pp. 335–368). Hillsdale, NJ: Lawrence Erlbaum Associates.

Zillmann, D. (1982). Television viewing and arousal. In D. Pearl, L. Bouthilet, & J. Lazar (Eds.), *Television and behavior: Ten years of scientific progress and implications for the eighties* (pp. 53–67). Washington, DC: U.S. Government Printing Office.

Zillmann, D. (1991). Television viewing and psychological arousal. In J. Bryant & D. Zillmann (Eds.), *Responding to the screen: Reception and reaction processes* (pp. 103–133). Hillsdale, NJ: Lawrence Erlbaum Associates.

Zillmann, D., & Gibson, R. (1996). Evolution of the horror genre. In J. B. Weaver & R. Tamborini (Eds.), *Horror films: Current research on audience preferences and reactions* (pp. 15–32). Mahwah, NJ: Lawrence Erlbaum Associates.

Zillmann, D., Weaver, J. B., Mundorf, N., & Aust, C. F. (1986). Effects of an opposite-gender companion's affect to horror on distress, delight, and attraction. *Journal of Personality and Social Psychology, 51,* 586–594.

Zuckerman, M. (1979). *Sensation seeking: Beyond the optimal level of arousal.* New York: Wiley.

Zuckerman, M. (1996). Sensation seeking and the taste for vicarious horror. In J. B. Weaver & R. Tamborini (Eds.), *Horror films: Current research on audience preferences and reactions* (pp. 147–160). Mahwah, NJ: Lawrence Erlbaum Associates.

Author Index

Subject Index